Homemade Pâtisserie

Pastry Made Easy

Homemade Pâtisserie
Pastry Made Easy

NH
NEW
HOLLAND

Vincent Gadan & Michelle Guberina

I would like to dedicate this book to all the ladies out there, as you make the world turn around and made me become a pastry chef—you are my most loyal customers. Above all, thanks to my mum, Jacqueline Gadan, who went through thick and thin to support my dream and is my heroine in the kitchen. Merci Maman!

Vincent

www.vincentgadan.com

To my wonderful mother, Ann, who gives enduring love and support no matter what is happening in my hectic life and who brings fabulous food, much love and joy to our family table.

Michelle

www.patisse.com.au

Contents

INTRODUCTION

Growing up in a little village called Barizey, with a population of only 120 inhabitants, in the wine region of Burgundy in France, I would never have dreamt that one day I would be sitting here writing an introduction to my first cookbook in a land so far away from where I started. It's still totally unbelievable to me.

In France, food is a way of life—actually one could say it is a religion. Every Sunday my maman would cook up a storm for the family. We would sit down to eat around 1 p.m. and virtually eat, talk and laugh until the early evening—this wasn't just an occasional family gathering, it was every Sunday. There would be dishes such as oeufs en meurette or salade niçoise and of course Maman's famous crème caramel. Maman is without doubt my biggest inspiration to pastry and dessert making. She achieves perfection every time—impressive given she has no formal qualifications. Sunday lunches are a childhood memory that I love and always look forward to re-creating on my annual trip home.

Growing up, I wasn't really sure what I wanted to do with my life. I was named Vincent—after the patron saint of winemakers—so I think my papa had ideas early on that he wanted me to become a winemaker, especially given that his family worked in the wine industry all their lives. So at the tender age of fourteen, I went to a wine school in the famous village of Beaune and then worked in a vineyard for a year. To say that I hated it was a mild understatement; I just didn't have that connection with terroir and wine. The work was very physical and my lack of enthusiasm might have been because the temperature in Burgundy in winter can drop to minus 15 degrees—so no, winemaking was not for me.

So there I was, a young guy, loving the country experience, living in one of the best wine regions in the world but not wanting to be a winemaker—what was I going to do? I realised what I loved the most was being in a kitchen and creating, so I decided to follow my dream and Maman helped me find an apprenticeship in the nearby town of Chalon-Sur-Saône.

Thanks to Monsieur Jean Perrat I commenced my pastry apprenticeship—and yes, I was hooked, I knew straightaway that pastry was me from A to Z. Despite having to work six days a week, getting up at 3 a.m. Sunday morning and not having a social life, my passion for pastry was born. Once I completed my apprenticeship, I was lucky to work at amazing restaurants such as Lameloise in Chagny and with Jacques Maximin at Le Diamant Rose in St Paul De Vence.

In France at that time, all males were required to complete one year of military service and at eighteen I had the opportunity to spend a year in the French navy. I would be on board a ship working as a pastry chef. It was while travelling around the world that I decided to leave France and emigrate.

Thanks to the Ritz Carlton, who agreed to sponsor me, I was on my way. Over the years I have worked as a pastry chef in some well-known restaurants including Level 41, Bistro Moncur, Bayswater Brasserie and Restaurant VII. A career highlight was working for three years with the man who I consider to be a great French-born chef, Guillaume Brahimi—it was a fantastic opportunity.

After three years, it was time for a change and that was when I met Michelle Guberina who owned Patisse. Over two years we produced fabulous French-inspired desserts for the cafe, developed a cooking class program for any level of home cook, hosted gourmet food tours to France each year and made regular TV appearances. Michelle looked after everything behind the scenes which allowed me to do what I love most—to create and teach the art of pastry. The two of us may be opposites—Michelle the cool, unflustered business woman, me the rebel French pastry chef—yet together we made a great team.

This book is divided into chapters that each focus on a different type of dough—I have designed the recipes to be simple, with step by step instructions, so that they're easy for you to replicate at home.

Enjoy! Life is sweet.
Vincent

BEFORE YOU BEGIN

The key to successful pastry making is to not be scared of trying. Many steps can be done in advance and always remember to give yourself time and not to rush. We promise that nothing will beat the feeling of creating something to share with everybody that you love.

Dough resting
This is important for all doughs—they must be rested before use as flour contains gluten. Gluten is the muscle of the flour, if you overwork it, the dough will become elastic and lose its shape while baking. Do not rush the recipe, rather, respect the resting time as it is an important factor in the success of pastry making. The longer the dough rests, the better the result you will achieve.

Dough storing
Most doughs can be stored in the refrigerator for up to 3 days. However, doughs which contain yeast cannot stay in the refrigerator for more than 48 hours. The recipe will tell you which doughs cannot be stored.

Dough rolling
To roll doughs, allow yourself space and always remember to lightly flour your kitchen bench prior to any rolling. Keep the dough moving freely on the bench to avoid it sticking.

Dough prebaking and weights
To prebake, we use something surprisingly practical—foil filled with weights, as it won't break or put pressure on doughs when applied. Here's how it works—once the pastry has been placed inside its mould, unroll some foil over the pastry, then fill the foil with weights such as rice, lentils or beans. You

can also buy proper baking weights which can be purchased in specialty cake or hospitality stores. This prevents the dough from rising and losing its shape. After prebaking, always remember to remove the weights, then proceed to the next step.

Oven temperature and time of cooking

Throughout the book, we try to keep it simple so most recipes are baked at between 340°F (170°C/Gas Mark 3) to 345°F (175°C/Gas Mark 4). The temperature and time of baking may vary depending on your oven and its capacity. Most recipes will ask you to preheat the oven—this is necessary otherwise the oven will drop too far in temperature when you are baking, which can result in a poor quality product.

Baked product shelf life

The recipe will direct you as to the shelf life of baked and unbaked doughs. Many of the doughs can be frozen unbaked; however, most recipes are best consumed within four hours of baking to guarantee freshness and flavour. Although the freezer is a great tool, nothing tastes as good as freshly baked product.

EQUIPMENT

Baking paper	Silicon mats can be substituted—they are more expensive, will last for years if cared for correctly
Baking tray	Standard to suit your oven
Blender	Can be a hand-held stick blender or food processor
Blowtorch	For caramelising sugar
Cake board	8in (20cm) diameter
Cake tin	9½in (24cm) diameter
Casserole dish	Rectangular with lid, about 12in (30cm) x 9½in (24cm)
Chopping board	Standard size
Plastic wrap	Standard size roll
Cooling rack	Oven tray size to cool baked products
Corer	To remove the cores from fruits such as apples and pears
Cutter	Round—1¼in (3cm), 1¾in (4cm), 2½in (6cm), 2¾in (7cm), 3¼in (8cm), 3½in (9cm), 4in (10cm), 5½in (13cm), 6in (15cm), 7in (18cm)
Cutter	Shaped, for gingerbread people
Digital thermometer	Measures temperature
Display stand	10in (25cm) diameter
Electric mixer	With hook, whisk and paddle attachments
Foam cone	To assemble croquembouche—4½in (11.5cm) diameter base x 10in (25cm) high
Frying pan	Diameter—8in (20cm), 10in (25cm), 12in (30cm)
Grater	Standard
Knife	3¼in (8cm) blade, 8in (20cm) blade, bread knife
Loaf tin	10in (25cm) x 3½in (9cm) x 3¼in (8cm)
Metal fruit horn	5½in (13cm) high x 1¾ (4.5cm) diameter cone
Metal ruler	Approximately 12in (30cm) long
Mixing bowls	4in (10cm) diameter, 8in (20cm) diameter
Muffin mould	2¾in (7cm) diameter x 1¾in (4cm) high
Mould	Kouglof—9in (22cm) diameter
Mould	Savarin—9in (22cm) round
Mould	Rectangular—5in (12cm) x 2½in (6cm) x 1¾in (4cm)
Palette knife	For lifting

Paper towel	For draining fried pastry
Pastry brush	Standard size
Peeler	For peeling fruit
Pie tins	4in (10cm) diameter x 1½in (3.5cm), aluminium
Piping bag	To pipe doughs and decorations
Piping nozzle	Star, no. 828
Piping nozzle	Ribbon, no. 808 (25mm)
Piping nozzle	Round—no. 801 (5mm), no. 803 (8mm), no. 804 (12mm), no. 805 (14mm), no. 806 (17mm)
Pizza trays	12in (30cm) diameter
Quiche mould	11in (27cm) diameter x 1¼in (3cm) deep
Rings	3in (7.5cm) diameter x 2in (5cm) high
Roasting tray	8in (20cm) x 12in (30cm) rectangle
Rolling pin	Standard size
Saucepan	6in (15cm) diameter, 8in (20cm) diameter, 9in (22cm) diameter all with a minimum 5in (12cm) depth—do not use Teflon-coated pans
Scraper	To scrape sides of mixing bowl
Sieve	Fine mesh, for straining
Skewers	To test readiness
Slotted spoon	Large serving spoon with holes commonly used for straining
Flexible spatula	To scrape sides of bowl
Springform tin	8in (20cm) x 2¾in (6.5cm) diameter
Tablespoons	For spooning mixture
Tart mould	4in (10cm) diameter x 1in (2.5cm) deep, fluted
Tart mould	8in (20cm) diameter x 1½in (3.5cm) deep
Tart mould	3¾in (9cm) diameter x ¾in (2cm) deep
Tart mould	11in (27cm) diameter x 1¼in (3cm) deep, fluted
Tartlet mould	2½in (6cm) diameter x ¾in (2cm) deep
Weights	For prebaking
Whisk	Standard size
Wooden spoon	For stirring
Wooden stick	Creating cavities in choux pastry

Sweet Dough

Pâte Sucrée

SWEET DOUGH
Pâte Sucrée

MAKES 12½OZ (370G)

Pâte sucrée, known as sweet dough, is a rich, buttery and sweet pastry. It is widely used in pastry kitchens as it is easy to work with, less crumbly than a sable dough and, due to a lower butter content, is ideal for liquid based tarts such as lemon tart and crème brûlée tart.

3oz (90g) unsalted butter, room temperature

1¾oz (50g) superfine/caster sugar

1 teaspoon vanilla essence

2 pinches table salt

1 egg (1¾–2oz/50–55g)

5½oz (160g) all-purpose/plain flour

²/3oz (20g) ground almonds

EQUIPMENT

Mixing bowl, 8in (20cm) diameter

Plastic wrap

Rolling pin

Baking weights

1. In a mixing bowl, place the butter, sugar, vanilla essence and salt.

2. Using one hand to hold the bowl steady, mix the ingredients together with your other hand until it forms a paste style consistency.

3. Add the egg, flour and ground almond to the mix, continue mixing until a dough is formed.

4. Wrap the dough in plastic wrap, flatten it out into a disc approximately ½in (1cm) thickness, then rest in the refrigerator for at least 20 minutes before using—this chills the dough and helps the rolling process.

5. Remove the dough from the refrigerator. Lightly flour a work area on your kitchen benchtop. Using a rolling pin, roll the dough to ⅛in (3mm) to ¼in (5mm) thickness, then cut to size, according to the recipe. Occasionally lift the dough from the bench and reflour to ensure the dough does not stick to the bench.

6. Once lined in the mould, place in baking weights (see Before You Begin) and bake at 345°F (175°C/Gas Mark 4) for approximately 20 minutes. Remember to remove weights after baking. The dough can be stored in the refrigerator for up to 3 days or frozen for 1 month.

TIPS AND TRICKS

The dough should roll easily with no cracking. The best way to avoid sticking is to roll quickly.

The pastry should be tender and crumbly when baked.

Most moulds do not require greasing; however, we highly recommend doing so as a precaution, to ensure a quality end-product. The best way is to brush with melted butter followed by a light coating of flour, or lightly spray with oil before lining with pastry.

PEAR BOURDALOUE
Poire Bourdaloue

ROUND
SERVES 5 TO 6

This classic pear and almond tart is said to have been created in a pâtisserie in Rue Bourdaloue in Paris in the early 1900s—more than a century later you can still visit that pâtisserie today.

ALMOND CREAM

¾oz (25g) unsalted butter, softened, room temperature

¾oz (25g) superfine/caster sugar

1 egg (1¾–2oz/50–55g)

1½oz (40g) ground almonds

1/6oz (5g) all-purpose/plain flour

2/3fl oz (20ml) rum

POACHED PEARS

4 Corella pears, small to medium, firm

48fl oz (1.5L) water

5oz (150g) superfine/caster sugar

3 cloves

6 bay leaves

15 black peppercorns, whole

grated zest of 1 orange

TART BASE

softened butter for greasing

flour for dusting

1 quantity (12½oz/370g) Sweet Dough (see recipe)

2 teaspoons honey, room temperature

1¾oz (50g) confectioner's/icing sugar for dusting

1. POACH THE PEARS

Peel and core the pears and cut in half, as this will accelerate cooking time, then set aside. In a saucepan, add the water, sugar, cloves, bay leaves, black peppercorns and grated orange, then bring to the boil. Reduce the heat so the poaching liquid is simmering then add the pears. Cover ingredients with a piece of baking paper; then place a saucer on top of the paper to keep the pears submerged beneath the liquid. Continue cooking until the fruit is soft when pierced with a knife, 20–40 minutes depending on the ripeness of the fruit. Remove the pan from the heat and leave the fruit in the poaching liquid to further infuse the aromas of the mixture. Set aside at room temperature until the pears are easy to handle, about 1 hour.

2. MAKE THE ALMOND CREAM FILLING

In a mixing bowl, place the softened butter and sugar, and mix with a whisk until all the sugar has been incorporated into the butter and it lightens in colour. This should take approximately 30 seconds. Add the egg, ground almond, flour then rum, and mix with the whisk until combined. Refrigerate for at least 20 minutes before using. The almond cream filling can be stored in the refrigerator for 3 days and frozen for up to 1 month.

3. PREPARE THE TART BASE

Prepare the tart mould by brushing inside with softened butter, dust with flour and shake off any excess. This will ensure the dough doesn't stick to the mould after baking. Lightly flour a clean surface on your kitchen bench, take the plastic wrap off the dough and place the dough in the centre of the work area. Using

a rolling pin, roll out the dough into a 10in (25cm) diameter circle. Gently wrap the dough around the rolling pin, then slowly unwind the dough over the mould. Starting from the centre, press in the dough lightly with your fingers, working your way around the base and then up the sides, making sure the bottom edge is in contact with the tart mould. Take the rolling pin and roll over the top of the mould—this will cut the top edges, giving you a clean finish. Rest in the refrigerator for 20–30 minutes.

Preheat the oven to 340°F (170°C/Gas Mark 3). Prepare the tart base with baking weights (see Before You Begin). Bake the base for 15–20 minutes.

4. ASSEMBLE, BAKE AND SERVE

Take the pears out of their juice and place on paper towels to remove excess syrup, then set aside. Once the tart case is baked, place the almond cream in the case and smooth out to spread evenly on the base. Arrange the 8 pear halves on top of the almond cream (flat side down). Place the tart in the middle of the oven and bake at 340°F (170°C/Gas Mark 3) for about 25 minutes or until golden in colour. Remove from the oven and allow to cool for 10 minutes before unmoulding.

Drizzle the top with some honey and dust with confectioner's sugar. Serve within 4 hours at room temperature.

EQUIPMENT

Saucepan, 9in (22cm) diameter x 5in (12cm) deep

Mixing bowl, 8in (20cm) diameter

Tart mould, 8in (20cm) diameter x 1½in (3.5cm) deep

Rolling pin

Baking weights

Baking tray

Whisk

Corer

Peeler

Baking paper

Plastic wrap

Paper towel

Knife, 3¼ in (8cm)

Saucer

TIPS AND TRICKS

Any stone fruit can be substituted for pears in the poaching mixture. The poaching time may vary based on the ripeness of the fruit.

NORMANDY APPLE TART
Tarte Normande

ROUND
SERVES 4 TO 6

This classic apple tart from Normandy in the north of France is a dish we always include in our cooking classes when we take tours to this region.

4 Granny Smith apples, small to medium

4¹/₃oz (130g) superfine/caster sugar

²/₃oz (20g) unsalted butter

3½fl oz (100ml) pouring cream

1 egg (1¾–2oz/50–55g)

1 egg yolk

TART BASE

softened butter for greasing

flour for dusting

1 quantity (12½oz/370g) Sweet Dough
    (see recipe)

1. PREPARE THE TART BASE

Prepare the tart mould by brushing inside with softened butter, dust with flour and shake off any excess. This will ensure the dough doesn't stick to the mould after baking. Lightly flour a clean surface on your kitchen bench, take the plastic wrap off the dough and place the dough in the centre of the work area. Using a rolling pin, roll out the dough into a 25cm (10in) diameter circle. Gently wrap the dough around the rolling pin, then slowly unwind the dough onto the mould. Starting from the centre, press in the dough lightly against all the edges, with your fingers, so there are no air pockets in the corners to ensure the mould is lined evenly. Work your way around the base and then up the sides, making sure the bottom edge is in contact with the tart mould. Take the rolling pin and roll over the top of the mould— this will cut the top edges, giving you a clean finish. Rest in the refrigerator for 20–30 minutes.

Preheat the oven to 345°F (175°C/Gas Mark 4). Prepare the tart base with baking weights (see Before you Begin). Bake the base for 20 minutes.

2. MAKE THE CARAMEL APPLE FILLING

Peel and core the apples, cut each into 8 wedges—32 wedges in total—then set aside. Sprinkle the sugar in the frying pan to cover the base, and place on the stovetop over medium heat. Stir continuously with a wooden spoon—the sugar will start to melt and eventually caramelise. When it reaches a dark honey colour, carefully add the apple wedges and the butter. Continue stirring to ensure all the wedges become coated with the caramel, and cook until the apple wedges are al dente (see Glossary). Using a

EQUIPMENT

Tart mould, 8in (20cm) diameter x 1½in (3.5cm) deep

Frying pan, 12in (30cm) diameter

Mixing bowls, 8in (20cm) diameter

Plastic wrap

Rolling pin

Baking weights

Plate

Peeler

Corer

Knife

Wooden spoon

Fine mesh sieve

sieve over a bowl (see Glossary), drain the apple wedges then set aside on a plate to cool.

Combine the cream with the caramel mixture in the bowl. In a separate bowl lightly beat the egg and egg yolk, then add to the caramel mix, stirring until combined well.

3. ASSEMBLE, BAKE AND SERVE

Arrange cooked apple wedges in the mould over the tart base and pour in the caramel filling to the rim. Bake at 340°F (170°C/ Gas Mark 3) for about 20 minutes—the tart is ready when it turns a light golden colour and the liquid is set. Remove the tart from the oven and let it rest for 10 minutes before unmoulding. Serve with a good quality vanilla ice cream.

CRÈME BRÛLÉE TART

Tarte Crème Brûlée

INDIVIDUAL
MAKES 4

The English and Spanish have both laid claim to creating crème brûlée; however, the French are without doubt the masters. If you want to caramelise the tops of these tarts, you will need a blowtorch.

1. PREPARE THE TART BASE

Prepare the tart moulds by brushing inside with softened butter, dust with flour and shake off any excess. Lightly flour a clean surface on your kitchen bench, take the plastic wrap off the dough and place the dough in the centre of the work area. Using a rolling pin, roll out dough and, using a cutter, cut 4 circles 5½in (13cm) diameter. Press the dough into the tart moulds, making sure the dough is in contact with the base and sides of the mould. Rest in refrigerator before baking.

Preheat the oven to 345°F (175°C/Gas Mark 4). Prepare the tart bases with baking weights (see Before you Begin). Bake the bases for 20 minutes. Remove the baking weights and set tart bases aside to cool; do not unmould.

2. MAKE THE FILLING

In a saucepan, place the cream with the scraped vanilla bean and bring to boiling point (see Glossary). In a mixing bowl, mix the egg yolks with the superfine sugar and whisk until light and pale in colour, approximately 30 seconds. Once the cream has come to the boil, add to the egg mixture, whisking consistently. Whisk the mixture for a few seconds more, then let it rest for 1 minute. Skim the top to remove the bubbles from the mixture (see Glossary).

16fl oz (450ml) pouring cream

1 vanilla bean, scraped (see Glossary)

9 egg yolks

2½ oz (75g) superfine/caster sugar

1.5 tablespoons raw sugar or superfine/caster
  sugar to caramelise

TART BASE

softened butter for greasing

flour for dusting

1 quantity (12½oz/370g) Sweet Dough
  (see recipe)

Sweet Dough

3. Assemble, bake and serve

Preheat the oven to 250°F (120°C/Gas Mark ½). Place the tart bases in their moulds on a baking tray. Carefully divide the egg filling between the tarts. Place the tray in the oven then top up with the egg filling so the bases are filled right to the top. Bake for approximately 40 minutes—when you shake the tart, the centre should be slightly wobbly. Remove from the oven and allow to cool, then store in the refrigerator until set, which may take up to 1 hour.

Unmould the tarts. If you wish to caramelise the tarts, sprinkle raw or superfine/caster sugar over the top. Using a blowtorch (see Glossary), move the flame consistently around the sugar so that it begins to melt and becomes a honey colour. Serve the tarts immediately as the crunch on the top will fade away after 20 minutes.

TIPS AND TRICKS

Use the wobble test to see if the brûlée is cooked—when you move the tray, the inside of the tart should wobble slightly and is not fully set.

The tart can be stored in the refrigerator overnight if the top has not been caramelised.

EQUIPMENT

4 tart moulds, fluted—4in (10cm) diameter x 1in (2.5cm) deep

Cutter, round, 5½in (13cm) diameter

Saucepan, 8in (20cm) diameter

Plastic wrap

Baking weights

Rolling pin

Mixing bowls, 8in (20cm)

Whisk

Blowtorch—see Glossary

Baking tray

Tablespoon

Sweet Dough

BAKED LEMON TART
Tarte au Citron

ROUND, LARGE
SERVES 5 TO 6

Every French mother and quality pâtisserie in France will make a classic tarte au citron—say no more.

9fl oz (250ml) pouring cream

grated zest of 2 lemons

7fl oz (200ml) lemon juice (about 8 lemons)

8 egg yolks

7oz (200g) superfine/caster sugar

TART BASE

softened butter for greasing

flour for dusting

1 quantity (12½oz/370g) Sweet Dough

   (see recipe)

1. PREPARE THE TART BASE

Prepare the tart mould by brushing inside with softened butter, dust with flour and shake off any excess. This will ensure the dough doesn't stick to the mould after baking. Lightly flour a clean surface on your kitchen bench, remove plastic wrap from the dough and place the dough in the centre of the work area. Using a rolling pin, roll out the dough into a 10in (25cm) diameter circle. Gently wrap the dough around the rolling pin, then slowly unwind the dough over the mould. Starting from the centre, press in the dough lightly with your fingers, working your way around the base and then up the sides, making sure the bottom edge is in contact with the tart mould. Take the rolling pin and roll over the top of the mould—this will cut the top edges, giving you a clean finish. Rest in the refrigerator for 20–30 minutes.

Preheat the oven to 340°F (170°C/Gas Mark 3). Prepare the tart base with baking weights (see Before you Begin). Bake the base for 15–20 minutes.

2. MAKE THE LEMON FILLING

In a saucepan, add the cream, grated lemon and lemon juice then place on the stovetop over medium heat and bring to boiling point. Meanwhile, in a mixing bowl, whisk the egg yolks and sugar until combined—the colour of the mix should be a little lighter—then set aside. Add cream mixture gradually into the egg mixture while whisking; continue to whisk for 30 seconds or until well combined. Sieve (see Glossary) the mixture into a bowl then let it rest for 1 minute. Remember to skim the top of the mixture (see Glossary).

3. ASSEMBLE, BAKE AND SERVE

Preheat the oven to 195°F (90°C/Gas Mark ½). Put the prebaked mould onto a baking tray and pour the lemon filling into the tart base. It is easier if you place the tray with the mould in the oven then pour the mixture in, as this will help reduce spilling. Bake for about 40–60 minutes—when you shake the tart, the centre should be slightly wobbly. Remove from the oven, then let it rest in the refrigerator for 1 hour before serving. It can be kept for up to 2 days in the refrigerator.

EQUIPMENT

Tart mould, 8in (20cm) diameter x 1½in (3.5cm) deep

Saucepan, 8in (20cm) diameter

Mixing bowls, 8in (20cm) diameter

Baking weights

Grater

Whisk

Sieve

Baking tray

Rolling pin

Tablespoon

TIPS AND TRICKS

Don't leave the sugar resting on top of the yolks without mixing together; this will cause the eggs to break down, making them less likely to thicken and set.

MERINGUE TOPPING FOR LEMON MERINGUE TART

Meringuée pour Tarte au Citron

This recipe is a classic meringue to top any lemon tart.

Place the egg whites into the bowl of an electric mixer and use the whisk attachment. Start to beat the whites at full speed. When the egg whites reach a soft peak, add the sugar in 3 lots, mixing for 2 minutes between each sugar addition. Once all combined, mix for another 5 minutes at full speed. When the meringue mixture is glossy and thick, stop the mixer and, using a tablespoon, place the meringue on top of the lemon tart. You can caramelise (see Glossary) the top of the tart with a blowtorch or bake it in the oven at 350°F (180°C/Gas Mark 4) until it is a light brown colour.

3 egg whites
6oz (180g) superfine/caster sugar

EQUIPMENT
Electric mixer and whisk attachment
Tablespoon

33

CARAMELISED WALNUT TARTLET

Tartelettes aux Noix et au Caramel

PETIT FOUR SIZE
MAKES 20 MINI TARTLETS

Walnuts are a great source of nutrients and taste delicious, especially with the addition of salted caramel in these easy-to-prepare tartlets.

SALTED CARAMEL

Makes 19oz (565g)

3oz (90g) liquid glucose

8oz (225g) superfine/caster sugar

7fl oz (200ml) pouring cream

1½oz (40g) unsalted butter

1/3oz (10g) coarse sea salt or table salt

NUT MIX

1½oz (40g) honey

6oz (180g) walnuts, or any mixed nuts, roasted

TART BASE

softened butter for greasing

flour for dusting

1 quantity (12½oz/370g) Sweet Dough (see recipe)

1. PREPARE THE TART BASE

Prepare the tart moulds by brushing inside with softened butter, dust with flour and shake off any excess. This will ensure that the dough doesn't stick to the tins after baking. Lightly flour a clean surface on your kitchen bench, take the plastic wrap off the dough and place the dough in the centre of the work area. Using a rolling pin, roll out dough and, using the cutter, cut 20 circles 3¼in (8cm) diameter. Press the dough into the tart moulds, making sure the dough is in contact with the base and sides of the mould. Rest in refrigerator for 20–30 minutes.

Preheat the oven to 345°F (175°C/Gas Mark 4). Prepare the tart bases with baking weights (see Before you Begin). Bake the bases for 20 minutes. Remove the baking weights and set tart bases aside to cool; do not unmould.

2. PREPARE THE SALTED CARAMEL

Place glucose in the pan and then add the sugar. Place on the stovetop, on a medium heat, and gently stir with a wooden spoon. The sugar will slowly dissolve as you are stirring and the mixture will eventually start to change colour to a golden brown around the edges. Continue to stir until the entire mix has turned a strong golden colour, evenly throughout the mix.

Meanwhile, heat the cream in another saucepan. Once you have a caramel, remove the cream from the heat and add the heated cream in stages, stirring continuously with a whisk. Stir in the butter and salt then set aside. Take the caramel off the heat and while still warm stir in the honey and nuts. This mixture can be stored in an airtight container for 3 days at room temperature or 1 week in the refrigerator.

3. ASSEMBLE AND SERVE
Remove from the mould and pour 1oz (30g) of the caramel filling into each tartlet. Serve at room temperature.

EQUIPMENT

20 tartlet moulds—2½in (6cm) diameter x
   ¾in (2cm) deep

Cutter, round, 3¼in (8cm)

2 saucepans, 9in (22cm) diameter

Baking weights

Wooden spoon

Whisk

Rolling pin

Plastic wrap

Mixing bowls

Baking tray

Baking paper

CLASSIC BAKED CHEESECAKE

Gâteau au Fromage

ROUND
SERVES 6 TO 8

Ancient Greece takes credit for the creation of the cheesecake—a Greek physician by the name of Aegimus is said to have written a cheesecake cookbook in the fifth century BC.

CHEESECAKE FILLING

17½oz (500g) cream cheese, ricotta or goat's
   cheese, room temperature

3½oz (100g) superfine/caster sugar

½oz (15g) cornstarch/cornflour

½oz (15g) all-purpose/plain flour

2 eggs (1¾–2oz/50–55g each)

grated zest of ½ lemon

5fl oz (150ml) pouring cream

1½oz (40g) unsalted butter, melted

BISCUIT BASE

¾ quantity (7oz/200g) Sweet Dough
   (see recipe)

2oz (60g) unsalted butter, softened

1 teaspoon vanilla essence

1. PREPARE THE BISCUIT BASE

Preheat the oven to 345°F (175°C/Gas Mark 4). Using a rolling pin, roll the dough to a ¼in (5mm) thickness. Place on a baking tray lined with baking paper and bake for 15–20 minutes. Let cool to room temperature.

Place the baked sweet dough into a mixing bowl and start crushing it by hand to resemble a rough sandy consistency. Place 2oz (60g) unsalted butter and vanilla essence into the crushed mixture and, using your fingertips, mix until a dough is formed. Line a springform tin with baking paper, press the biscuit base evenly over the bottom of the tin and bake for 15 minutes. Set aside at room temperature to cool.

2. PREPARE THE CHEESECAKE FILLING

In a electric mixer with a whisk attachment, combine the cheese and sugar, mixing continuously until combined. Add in the cornstarch, all-purpose flour, eggs and grated lemon, then gradually add the pouring cream and melted butter. Turn off the mixer, scrape the sides of the bowl and mix again to combine well.

3. Assemble, bake and serve

Pour the filling mixture straight into the prepared biscuit base. Bake at 340°F (170°C/Gas Mark 3) for 25 minutes or more—the mixture should be set to a wobbly consistency. Allow to cool completely. Remove from the mould and serve at room temperature or chilled.

EQUIPMENT

Springform tin, 8in (20cm) x 2¾in (6.5cm)

Mixing bowls, 8in (20cm) diameter

Plastic wrap

Rolling pin

Electric mixer and whisk attachment

Scraper

Whisk

Baking tray

Baking paper

TIPS AND TRICKS

Make sure the cream cheese is at room temperature, otherwise it will not develop a creamy consistency and will have lumps throughout the mix.

NEW YORK PASSIONFRUIT CHEESECAKE

Cheesecake de New York au Fruit de la Passion

ROUND
SERVES 6 TO 8

A New York cheesecake relies on heavier cheeses such as cream cheese and sour cream as part of its ingredients. In New York in 1929, a restaurant owner named Arnold Reuben laid claim to inventing this heavier style cheesecake.

1. PREPARE THE BISCUIT BASE

Preheat the oven to 345°F (175°C/Gas Mark 4). Using a rolling pin, roll the dough to a ¼in (5mm) thickness. Place on a lined baking tray and bake for 12 minutes. Let cool to room temperature.

Place the baked sweet dough into a mixing bowl and start crushing it by hand to resemble a rough sandy consistency. Remove one-third and set aside for decoration. Place 2oz (60g) unsalted butter and vanilla essence into the crushed mixture and, using your fingertips, mix until a dough is formed. Line a springform tin with baking paper, press the biscuit base evenly over the bottom of the tin and bake for 15 minutes. Set aside to cool.

2. MAKE THE CHEESECAKE FILLING

Soak the gelatine leaves in cold water to soften and then drain. Using the electric mixer with a paddle attachment, combine the cream cheese and sour cream with the sugar. Mix 2 tablespoons passionfruit puree with soaked and drained gelatine in a small saucepan over low heat, so that everything melts together and no lumps appear. Stir into the cream cheese mixture with the rest of the passionfruit puree.

3. ASSEMBLE, BAKE AND SERVE

Pour the filling mixture straight into the prepared biscuit base. Place in the refrigerator until set to a wobbly consistency. Remove from the mould and serve at room temperature.

1/6oz (6g) gelatine leaves

17½oz (500g) cream cheese, at room temperature

5oz (140g) sour cream

4oz (120g) superfine/caster sugar

3oz (90g) passionfruit puree

BISCUIT BASE

1 quantity (12½oz/370g) Sweet Dough (see recipe)

2oz (60g) unsalted butter

1 teaspoon vanilla essence

EQUIPMENT

Baking paper

Springform tin, 8in (20cm) x 2¾in (6.5cm)

Plastic wrap

Rolling pin

Electric mixer and paddle attachment

Saucepan, 6in (15cm)

Mixing bowl, 8in (20cm) diameter, to soak gelatine

Flexible spatula

Whisk

Tablespoon

Sweet Dough

Pie Dough

Pâte Brisée

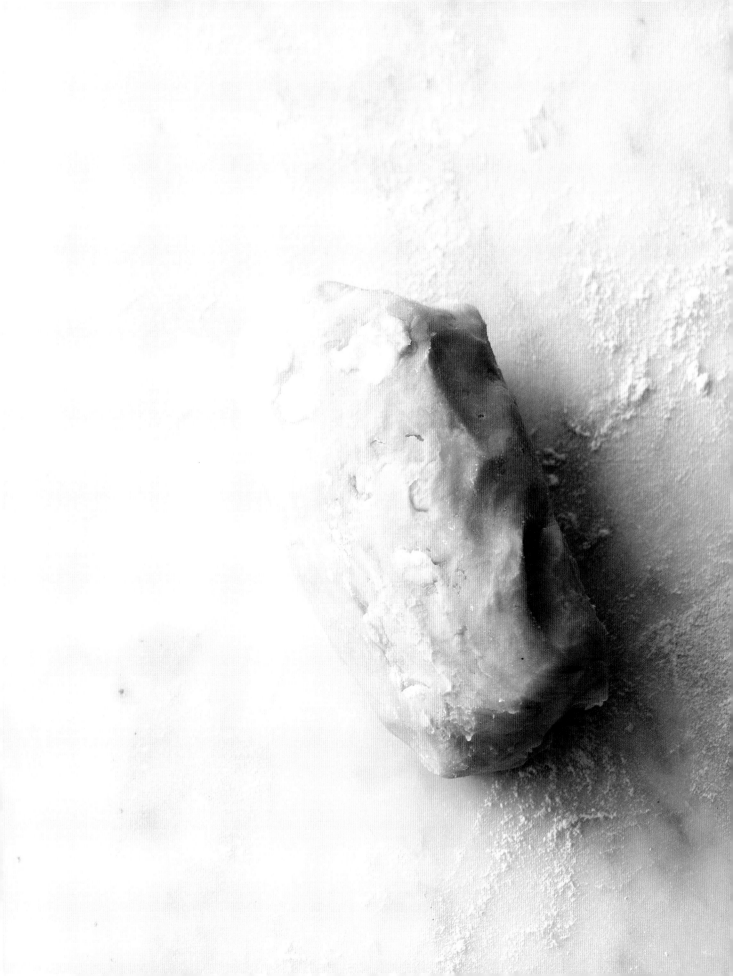

PIE DOUGH
Pâte Brisée

MAKES 16OZ (460G)

This versatile dough is a crumbly pastry used for mainly savoury items such as pies and quiches. It can also be used for sweet desserts such as Flan Parisien.

6oz (180g) unsalted butter, cold, diced ⅔in (1.5cm) cubes

8oz (230g) all-purpose/plain flour

2 pinches table salt

1¾fl oz (50ml) water

EQUIPMENT
Mixing bowl, 8in (20cm) diameter
Rolling pin
Baking tray
Plastic wrap
Baking weights

TIPS AND TRICKS
If making the dough with an electric mixer, use a paddle attachment and stop regularly to check that the butter is not overmixed.

1. In a bowl, rub the butter into the flour and salt until it forms a crumbly texture—there should still be partial chunks of butter in the dry mix.

2. Add the water and mix until just combined—the butter should still be seen in the dough like a marbled effect. Do not overwork or you will lose the crumbly texture and layering effect of the butter.

3. Flatten the dough into a rectangle approximately ¼in (1cm) thick, wrap it in plastic wrap and rest the dough in the refrigerator for 20 minutes.

4. Lightly flour a clean surface on your kitchen bench. Take out the dough from the refrigerator, remove the plastic wrap and, using a rolling pin, roll out to a ⅛in (3mm) thickness—lift up the dough from the bench occasionally to relax it, and re-flour if needed to ensure the dough is not sticking to the bench. Then cut to size according to the recipe and place in a tart mould.

5. Preheat the oven to 340°F (170°C/Gas Mark 3). Prepare the tart base with baking weights (see Before you Begin). Bake for about 20–25 minutes. The dough can be stored in the refrigerator for up to 3 days or frozen for 1 month.

CUSTARD TART
Flan Parisien

LARGE
SERVES 4 TO 6

We love this flan so much—when we are in Paris on our French tour, we look for it every day as our treat.

13fl oz (400ml) milk

2¾fl oz (100ml) pouring cream

1 vanilla bean, scraped (see Glossary)

5 egg yolks

3½ oz (100g) superfine/caster sugar

¾oz (25g) cornstarch/cornflour

TART BASE

softened butter for greasing

flour for dusting

¾ quantity (10½oz/300g) Pie Dough
   (see recipe)

1. PREPARE THE TART BASE

Prepare the tart mould by brushing inside with softened butter, dust with flour and shake off any excess. This will ensure the dough doesn't stick to the mould after baking. Lightly flour a clean surface on your kitchen bench, remove plastic wrap from the dough and place the dough in the centre of the work area. Using a rolling pin, roll out the dough into a 10in (25cm) diameter circle. Gently wrap the dough around the rolling pin, then slowly unwind the dough over the mould. Starting from the centre, press in the dough lightly with your fingers, working your way around the base and then up the sides. Take the rolling pin and roll over the top of the mould—this will cut the top edges, giving you a clean finish. Rest the dough in the refrigerator for 20 minutes.

Preheat the oven to 340°F (170°C/Gas Mark 3). Prepare the tart base with baking weights (see Before you Begin). Bake the base for 20–25 minutes.

2. PREPARE THE FILLING

In a small saucepan, pour in the milk and cream. Cut the vanilla bean lengthways and scrape out the seeds with a knife (see Glossary). Add the seeds and pod to the saucepan and bring to the boil. In a mixing bowl, whisk the egg yolks and sugar, then add cornstarch. When the milk mixture comes to the boil, pour into the egg mixture and continue whisking vigorously. Pour the mixture back into the saucepan, place on the stovetop over a medium heat and continue whisking until the custard comes to the boil. Continue to whisk and cook the custard for 1 minute, then remove the saucepan from the heat and continue whisking for another 30 seconds. Remove the vanilla bean skins.

EQUIPMENT

Tart mould, 8in (20cm) diameter x 1½in
  (3.5cm) deep, fluted

Saucepan, 8in (20cm) diameter

Small knife for scraping vanilla

Plastic wrap

Baking weights

Rolling pin

Mixing bowls, 8in (20cm) diameter

Whisk

3. ASSEMBLE, BAKE AND SERVE

Pour the mixture into the prebaked tart base. Bake at 345°F (175°C/Gas Mark 4) for 20 minutes or until the top changes colour. Set in the refrigerator for about 1 hour. Serve chilled or at room temperature—the flan can be stored in the refrigerator for two days.

BACON AND EGG QUICHE
Quiche Lorraine

ROUND
SERVES 5 TO 6

The word 'quiche' is said to have originated from the German word 'kuchen' which actually means cake. Serve this with salad and tomato relish.

1. PREPARE THE QUICHE BASE

Prepare the tart mould by brushing inside with softened butter, dust with flour and shake off any excess. This will ensure the dough doesn't stick to the mould after baking. Lightly flour a clean surface on your kitchen bench, remove plastic wrap from the dough and place the dough in the centre of the work area. Using a rolling pin, roll out the dough into a 12in (30cm) diameter circle. Roll onto a rolling pin and then slowly unwind the dough over the mould. Starting from the centre, press in the dough lightly over the bottom of the tin with your fingers, working your way around the base and then up the sides. Roll the rolling pin over the top of the mould—this will cut the top edges, giving you a clean finish. Rest in refrigerator for 20 minutes before baking.

Preheat the oven to 345°F (175°C/Gas Mark 4). Prepare the tart base with baking weights (see Before you Begin). Bake for 20–25 minutes.

2. PREPARE THE QUICHE FILLING

In a heavy frying pan over medium to high heat, sauté the bacon in the vegetable oil until golden brown. Remove from the heat and set aside to cool. In a mixing bowl, whisk the eggs, cream, milk and salt until combined.

3. ASSEMBLE, BAKE AND SERVE

Place the bacon into the prebaked case then cover with cheese. Pour in the egg mix to the rim of the quiche and add cracked pepper on top. Try not to spill any over the sides of the pastry, which will make removing the mould difficult. Bake at 340°F (170°C/Gas Mark 3) for 25–30 minutes; it should be slightly wobbly in the centre when ready. Let it rest for 5–10 minutes, then remove gently from mould.

9½oz (270g) bacon, diced

1½ tablespoons extra virgin olive oil

3 eggs (1¾–2oz/50–55g each)

4fl oz (120ml) pouring cream

4fl oz (120ml) milk

2 pinches salt

cracked black pepper

3½ oz (100g) cheese, shredded

QUICHE BASE

softened butter for greasing

flour for dusting

¾ quantity (10½oz/300g) Pie Dough
(see recipe)

EQUIPMENT

Tart mould, 11in (27cm) diameter, 1¼in
(3cm) deep, fluted

Frying pan, heavy, 8in (20cm) diameter

Mixing bowl, 8in (20cm) diameter

Rolling pin

Plastic wrap

Baking weights

Whisk

Knife

Chopping board

Wooden spoon

Pie Dough

PROVINCIAL QUICHE

Quiche Provençale

ROUND
SERVES 5 TO 6

This quiche always features delicious ripe tomatoes conjuring aromas from Provence in the South of France.

1 large red bell pepper/capsicum, seeded and
  diced ¾in (2cm)

1 large yellow bell pepper/capsicum, seeded and
  diced ¾in (2cm)

1 zucchini/courgette, medium, cut in half
  lengthways and sliced finely

1½ tablespoons extra virgin olive oil

2 sprigs fresh thyme, chopped

2 garlic cloves, chopped finely

4 Roma tomatoes, quartered

salt and cracked pepper to taste

3 eggs (1¾–2oz/50–55g each)

5fl oz (150ml) pouring cream

5fl oz (150ml) milk

3½ oz (100g) feta, drained and chopped

QUICHE BASE

softened butter for greasing

flour for dusting

¾ quantity (10½oz/300g) Pie Dough
  (see recipe)

1. PREPARE THE QUICHE BASE

Prepare the tart mould by brushing inside with softened butter, dust with flour and shake off any excess. This will ensure the dough doesn't stick to the mould after baking. Lightly flour a clean surface on your kitchen bench, remove plastic wrap from the dough and place the dough in the centre of the work area. Using a rolling pin, roll out the dough into a 12in (30cm) diameter circle. Roll onto a rolling pin and then slowly unwind the dough over the mould. Starting from the centre, press in the dough lightly with your fingers, working your way around the base and then up the sides, making sure the bottom edge is in contact with the mould. Take the rolling pin and roll over the top of the mould—this will cut the top edges, giving you a clean finish. Rest in refrigerator for 20 minutes before baking.

Preheat the oven to 345°F (175°C/Gas Mark 4). Prepare the tart base with baking weights (see Before you Begin). Bake the base for 30–40 minutes then remove from the oven and set aside.

2. PREPARE THE FILLING

Place the peppers and zucchini in a roasting tray and drizzle with olive oil. Scatter the thyme and garlic over the top then roast in the oven at 345°F (175°C/Gas Mark 4) for 15 minutes. Add the tomato and roast for another 10 minutes. Season to taste with salt and pepper, and set aside to cool.

In a mixing bowl, whisk the eggs, cream, milk and salt until combined.

3. ASSEMBLE, BAKE AND SERVE

Scatter the roasted vegetables over the base of the prebaked
mould, then sprinkle with the feta. Place the filled quiche base
onto a baking tray and pour in the filling mixture to the rim—
making sure that it doesn't overflow—then season with cracked
pepper. Bake in the oven at 340°F (170°C/Gas Mark 3) for 25–30
minutes. When the quiche is ready, it should be slightly wobbly
in the centre. Let it rest for 5–10 minutes, then remove from
mould gently—serve with green leaves and tomato relish.

WAGYU BEEF PIE
Tourte au Boeuf

ROUND
MAKES 6 INDIVIDUAL PIES

This is a pie that will be a winner with the family—lots of chunky wagyu beef and crispy pastry.

1. PREPARE THE PIE BASE

Prepare the pie tins by brushing inside with softened butter. Lightly flour a clean surface on your kitchen bench, remove plastic wrap from the dough and place the dough in the centre of the work area. Using a rolling pin, roll out the dough to about 12in (30cm) x 18in (45cm) in size, then cut 6 discs each 6in (15cm) diameter. Gently place a disc in the centre of each pie tin and press in the dough with your fingers, making sure the bottom edge is in contact with the tin. The rim can be left untrimmed. Rest in refrigerator for 20 minutes before baking.

Preheat the oven to 340°F (170°C/Gas Mark 3). Prepare the tart base with baking weights (see Before you Begin). Bake for 20 minutes then remove from the oven and set aside.

2. PREPARE THE PIE FILLING

Heat a casserole dish with 2 tablespoons of the vegetable oil. On a high heat, brown the wagyu for about 3–4 minutes, until the meat is browned well. Reduce to a medium heat and cook for a further 2 minutes, then remove from the dish and set aside. Add remaining 1 tablespoon vegetable oil to the dish and sweat the onions until translucent. Add carrots, leeks, celery and thyme, stirring for 3 minutes. Add the melted butter and flour and stir well. Finally, add the tomatoes, browned meat, red wine and beef stock. Cover the dish with a lid and bake at 340°F (170°C/Gas Mark 3) for 2 hours. The filling is ready when the meat is tender. Season to taste with salt and pepper. Mixture can be used straight away and can be stored for up to three days in the refrigerator.

Makes 23oz (640g) filling

3 tablespoons vegetable oil

17½oz (500g) wagyu or beef shin, diced into 1¼in (3cm) strips

1 brown onion, diced

1¾oz (50g) each celery, carrot and leek, diced into ½in (1cm)

¼ bunch fresh thyme, picked

1¼oz (35g) unsalted butter, melted

1¼oz (35g) all-purpose/plain flour

3 tomatoes, vine-ripened, diced into ¾in (2cm)

11fl oz (330ml) red wine

11fl oz (330ml) beef stock

salt and pepper to taste

1 egg for egg wash

1 quantity (24oz/675g) Puff Pastry (see recipe), cut into six 5in (12cm) discs, 1/ in (4mm) thick

PIE BASE

softened butter for greasing

2 quantities (32oz/920g) Pie Dough (see recipe)

Pie Dough

3. ASSEMBLE, BAKE AND SERVE

Fill each prebaked pie base with the beef mix to the rim—about 3¾oz (110g) of filling per pie base. Brush egg wash on the edge of each puff pastry disc. Flip over the puff pastry disc and place onto the pie base so that the egg wash joins the two pastries. Gently press the lid onto the pie base rim then cut a cross in the centre of the pie lid to allow steam to escape while cooking. Brush egg wash over the top of the lid to give it colour and gloss. Bake at 345°F (175°C/Gas Mark 4) for 20–30 minutes until the puff pastry lid is golden brown. Serve with green leaves and relish.

EQUIPMENT

Casserole dish, rectangular, 12in (30cm)
*   x 9½in (24cm), with lid*

6 pie tins, aluminium, 4in (10cm) diameter
*   x 1½in (3.5cm) deep*

Rolling pin

Plastic wrap

Cutter, 6in (15cm)

Baking weights

Pastry brush

Wooden spoon

Tablespoons

Rolling pin

Knife

Chopping board

Baking tray

TIPS AND TRICKS

The wagyu filling can be made in advance and frozen for up to 1 month. Defrost before using.

CHICKEN PIE

Tourte au Poulet

This is a variation on the beef pie. Use free-range chicken to achieve the best flavour results.

2 tablespoons vegetable oil

14oz (400g) chicken thigh fillet, diced into ¾in (2cm) cubes

1oz (30g) unsalted butter

2¼oz (70g) all-purpose/plain flour

2¼fl oz (70ml) pouring cream

8fl oz (230ml) chicken stock

2¾fl oz (100ml) white wine

1 leek, diced into ½in (1cm) cubes

1 celery stalk, diced into ½in (1cm) cubes

½ bunch fresh thyme, picked

salt and pepper to taste

1 egg for egg wash

1 quantity (24oz /675g) Puff Pastry (see recipe), cut into six 5in (12cm) discs, ¹/6in (4mm) thick

PIE BASE

softened butter for greasing

2 quantities (32oz/920g) Pie Dough (see recipe)

1. PREPARE THE PIE BASE

Prepare the pie tins by brushing inside with softened butter. Lightly flour a clean surface on your kitchen bench, remove plastic wrap from the dough and place the dough in the centre of the work area. Using a rolling pin, roll out the dough to about 12in (30cm) x 18in (45cm) in size, then cut 6 discs each 6in (15cm) diameter. Gently place a disc in the centre of each pie tin and press in the dough with your fingers, making sure the bottom edge is in contact with the tin. The rim can be left untrimmed. Rest in refrigerator for 20 minutes before baking.

Preheat the oven to 345°F (175°C/Gas Mark 4). Prepare the tart base with baking weights (see Before you Begin). Bake for 20 minutes then remove from the oven and set aside.

2. PREPARE THE PIE FILLING

Heat a large saucepan with the vegetable oil. Add the chicken and cook for 6–7 minutes until brown—remove chicken from the pan and set aside. Melt the butter in the same pan, then stir in flour. Add the cream, stock and white wine and continue to stir slowly until mixture has thickened. Add the vegetables, thyme and cooked chicken, then place a lid on the saucepan and cook over low heat for about 1 hour or until the vegetables are tender and the sauce has thickened. Season with salt and pepper to taste.

3. ASSEMBLE, BAKE AND SERVE

Fill each prebaked pie base with the chicken mix to the rim—about 3¾oz (110g) of filling per pie base. Cut a hole in the centre of the pie lid to allow steam to escape. Brush egg wash on the edge of each puff pastry disc. Flip over the puff pastry disc and place onto the pie base so that the egg wash joins the two pastries. Gently press the lid onto the pie base rim. Brush egg wash over the top of the lid to give it colour and gloss. Bake at 340°F (170°C/Gas Mark 3) for 30–40 minutes until the puff pastry lid is golden brown. Serve with green leaves and relish.

EQUIPMENT

Saucepan, 9in (22cm) diameter, with lid

Six pie tins, aluminium, 4in (10cm) diameter
   x 1½in (3.5cm) deep

Pastry brush

Rolling pin

Plastic wrap

Cutter, 6in (15cm)

Baking weights

Wooden spoon

Knife for chopping

Chopping board

Pie Dough

CANNOLI
Cannoli Siciliani

INDIVIDUAL
MAKES 20 MINI

Cannoli originate from Sicily in Italy—the word means 'little tube'. These are filled with a delicious ricotta filling. Crème pâtissière can be substituted for the ricotta if you prefer.

6½oz (190g) all-purpose/plain flour

½oz (15g) superfine/caster sugar

2½fl oz (85ml) Vermouth

1 pinch salt

48fl oz (1.5L) vegetable oil for frying

1¾oz (50g) pure confectioner's/icing sugar

RICOTTA FILLING

7oz (200g) ricotta, drained well

1/3oz (10g) roasted nuts, chopped

1/3oz (10g) glace fruit, chopped

½oz (15g) pure confectioner's/icing sugar, sifted

1/3fl oz (10ml) Cointreau or similar liqueur

EQUIPMENT

Mixing bowls, 8in (20cm) diameter

Rolling pin

Plastic wrap

Cutter, round, 3¼in (8cm)

Wooden spoon with a round handle

Saucepan, 9in (22cm) diameter

Fork

Slotted spoon

Paper towel

Piping bag

Piping nozzle no. 805

Flexible spatula

1. PREPARE THE CANNOLI DOUGH

Place the flour, sugar, vermouth and salt in a bowl, and mix to make a firm dough. Flatten the dough into a disc and wrap in plastic wrap. Rest in the refrigerator for 20 minutes. Using a rolling pin, roll out into a square, as thinly as possible. You should be able to see the shadow of your hand through the pastry. Cut out ten round pieces with the cutter. Lightly oil the wooden spoon to prevent sticking, then wrap one cannoli around the end of each spoon, not too tight. Seal the ends by lightly wetting and pressing the ends of the dough together. The dough can be rerolled and recut.

Place the saucepan with vegetable oil on the stovetop over a high heat—the oil should be at least 2½in (6cm) deep in the pan. Heat the oil to 325–340°F (160–175°C). Place one cannoli per wooden spoon into the oil. Cook for 2 minutes then, using the fork, slide the cannoli off the wooden spoon onto paper towel to drain. Allow to cool to room temperature. These shells can be stored in an airtight container for 3 days.

2. PREPARE THE RICOTTA FILLING

Mix all the filling ingredients together in a bowl until evenly combined.

3. ASSEMBLE AND SERVE

Place the ricotta filling in the piping bag with the piping nozzle. Fill each cannoli—about 2/3oz (20g) per cannoli, then dust with icing sugar. Serve immediately.

Pie Dough

DIJON CHEESE BISCUITS

Biscuit au Fromage de Dijon

A fabulous little cheesy biscuit that's easy to make ahead of time and perfect for a drinks party.

1. PREPARE THE BISCUIT DOUGH

Preheat the oven to 340°F (170°C/Gas Mark 3). Place all ingredients, except egg wash and extra parmesan, into the mixing bowl and mix until well combined. Flatten the dough into an 8in x 6in (20cm x 15cm) rectangle, wrap with plastic wrap and refrigerate for at least 20 minutes. Lightly flour the bench top and roll out the dough to a 12in x 8in (30cm x 20cm) rectangle. Refrigerate until firm, about 10 minutes. Lightly brush with egg wash and sprinkle the extra grated Parmesan on top. Cut the dough into 4in x ¾in (10cm x 2cm) strips.

2. BAKE AND SERVE

Place the strips, well spaced out, on a baking tray lined with baking paper. Bake for 10 minutes, then turn the tray around and bake for a further 8 minutes. Allow to cool. Store in an airtight container for up to 3 days.

5oz (150g) all-purpose/plain flour

1 egg (1¾–2oz/50–55g)

3¾oz (115g) unsalted butter, diced

5 pinches salt

3oz (90g) Parmesan, grated

1 pinch pepper

1 pinch baking powder

¹/₃oz (10g) Dijon mustard

1 egg for egg wash

extra Parmesan, grated

EQUIPMENT

Mixing bowl, 8in (20cm)

Wooden spoon

Plastic wrap

Knife

Rolling pin

Pastry brush

Baking tray

Baking paper

Pie Dough

PROVINCIAL SLICE

Pissaladière

MAKES 1 SLAB, 9IN X 8IN (22CM X 20CM)

Conjuring up dreams of the South of France, this speciality from Nice is a classic savoury pastry and is always garnished with anchovy. It can be served as a canapé or as a light meal.

1 quantity Pie Dough (see recipe)

flour for dusting

1¾fl oz (50ml) olive oil

3 brown onions, sliced ¼in (5mm)

1½oz (40g) unsalted butter

2 sprigs thyme leaves, chopped

16 anchovies, halved lengthwise

16 Kalamata olives, pitted and halved

EQUIPMENT

Mixing bowl, 8in (20cm) diameter

Rolling pin

Baking tray

Baking paper

Plastic wrap

Frying pan 8in (20cm) diameter

Cooling rack

Knife for cutting

Chopping board

Wooden spoon

1. PREPARE THE DOUGH

Make the dough following the recipe for Pie Dough (see recipe). Lightly flour the bench top and, using a rolling pin, roll the dough to a rectangle ½in (1cm) thick then transfer the dough to a baking tray lined with baking paper. Rest for 20 minutes in the refrigerator.

Preheat the oven to 340°F (170°C/Gas Mark 3). Bake the dough for 20–30 minutes or until golden brown. Allow to cool.

2. ASSEMBLE, BAKE AND SERVE

Heat olive oil in a frying pan over low heat and cook onions to a light brown colour. Stir in butter and thyme. Allow to cool.

Spread the onions over the dough, right up to the edges, then lay the anchovies in a criss-cross pattern on top of the onions. Place an olive half in the centre of each square formed by the anchovies. Bake the pissaladière at 350°F (180°C/Gas Mark 4) for 10 minutes then slide off the baking tray onto a cooling rack. Cut in large slices and serve warm immediately with a goat's cheese salad.

Biscuit Dough

Pâte Sablée

BISCUIT DOUGH
Pâte Sablée

MAKES 30OZ (840G)

*This biscuit dough has a higher butter content than sweet dough so it is ideal
for cookies or biscuits.*

13oz (375g) all-purpose/plain flour

1/3oz (10g) almond meal

7½oz (220g) unsalted butter, cold, diced ¼in
(5mm)

grated zest of ½ orange

½ vanilla bean, cut lengthways, scraped
(see Glossary)

2 pinches table salt

¼oz (8g) baking powder

5oz (150g) pure confectioner's/icing sugar

2 eggs (1¾–2oz/50–55g each)

EQUIPMENT

Baking weights

Mixing bowl, 8in (20cm)

Grater

Plastic wrap

Small knife for scraping vanilla

TIPS AND TRICKS

Using almond meal gives a more biscuit-
like texture and taste—if you have nut
allergies, replace the almond meal with
flour. Any flavour or spice can be used
instead of zest—try cinnamon, cardamom
or ground coffee.

1. Place flour, almond meal and cold butter into a mixing bowl and rub the ingredients between your hands until it forms a sandy texture.

2. Add the grated zest, vanilla seeds, salt, baking powder, sugar and whole eggs, then mix with one hand to make a dough ball. Mix for 2 minutes until all combined.

3. Flatten the dough into a rectangle. Wrap the dough in plastic wrap and refrigerate for at least 20 minutes before using. Remove from the refrigerator, set on the bench and cut according to the recipe.

4. Prepare the dough with baking weights (see Before you Begin) and bake the dough for 10–15 minutes. The dough can be stored in the refrigerator for up to 3 days or frozen for 1 month.

Biscuit Dough

BRITTANY BISCUIT
Biscuit Breton

MAKES 22 BISCUITS

Originating from Brittany in the northwest of France, these biscuits have a sandy-like texture and are traditionally round with fluted edges.

3½ oz (100g) unsalted butter, melted

3½ oz (100g) superfine/caster sugar

½ quantity (14½oz/420g) Biscuit Dough
   (see recipe)

EQUIPMENT

22 metal cake rings, 3in x 2in (7.5cm x 5cm)
   high

Palette knife

Baking tray

Baking paper

Rolling pin

1. Preheat the oven to 340°F (170°C/Gas Mark 3) and line a baking tray with baking paper.

2. Roll the dough between 2 sheets of baking paper to a thickness of about ¼in (5mm), then refrigerate the sheets for 5 minutes.

3. Grease the cake rings with the melted butter or lightly spray with oil. Rim one side of the buttered ring with the superfine/caster sugar.

4. Place the dough sheets on your kitchen bench, remove the top sheet of baking paper and, using the sugared rings, cut out discs—do not remove the rings. Using a palette knife, transfer the discs in the cake rings onto the baking tray. Spread out evenly, about ¾in (2cm) apart, to allow even heat distribution. The remaining dough can be pressed back together and rolled again, repeating steps 3 and 4.

5. Bake for 15–18 minutes. Remove from the oven and allow the tray to cool before removing rings. Biscuits can be stored in an airtight container for up to 3 days.

GLASSES BISCUIT
Lunettes de Romans

MAKES 10 BISCUITS

These biscuits get their name from the French word for reading glasses—lunette.

1. PREPARE THE BISCUIT DOUGH

Remove the plastic wrap from the dough and, using a rolling pin, roll between 2 sheets of baking paper to $1/8$in (3mm) thickness then let it rest in the refrigerator for 10 minutes. Remove the top sheet and, using a cutter, cut 20 discs. Using a spatula, carefully lift and place the discs on a baking tray lined with baking paper, allowing a ¾in (2cm) gap between each biscuit. Each oval should weigh about ⅔oz (20g). Using a piping nozzle, cut two 'eye' holes into every second biscuit.

2. BAKE, ASSEMBLE AND SERVE

Preheat the oven to 340°F (170°C/Gas Mark 3). Bake for 12–15 minutes until golden brown. Remove from the oven and allow to cool.

Turn the biscuits with no holes over and spread a thin layer of jelly, hazelnut paste or melted chocolate onto the flat side of the biscuit. Lightly dust sugar over the remaining discs with holes and place on top of the biscuits with the spread.

½ quantity (14½oz/420g) Biscuit Dough (see recipe)

3½ oz (100g) good quality jelly/jam (pulp free), hazelnut paste or melted chocolate

1¾oz (50g) confectioner's/icing sugar for dusting

EQUIPMENT

Cutter, oval, 5½in (13cm) diameter (round can be substituted)

Baking paper

Plastic wrap

Rolling pin

Flexible spatula

Small piping nozzle, to cut holes

Baking tray

Baking paper

Small knife

TIPS AND TRICKS

If it is difficult to source hazelnut paste, Nutella can be used as a substitute (reduce the quantity by half if using Nutella).

ICE CREAM SANDWICH
Sandwich de Crème Glacée

MAKES 11 SANDWICHES

A great way to incorporate pastry and ice cream for a relaxed summer dessert.

22 Brittany Biscuits (see recipe)

32fl oz (1L) ice cream of your choice

7oz (200g) nuts, crushed and roasted

EQUIPMENT

11 cake rings, 3in x 2in (7.5cm x 5cm) high

Tablespoon

Baking tray

TIPS AND TRICKS

Other coatings can be used instead of nuts,
such as chocolate chips, sprinkles, or crushed
nougatine

1. PREPARE THE BISCUITS

Make the biscuits following the recipe for Brittany Biscuits (see recipe).

2. ASSEMBLE AND SERVE

Place 1 biscuit, flat side down, into each of the 11 cake rings. Scoop 2 tablespoons of ice cream into each ring, pressing down so there are no air pockets. Fill the rings with ice cream to ¼in (5mm) from the top of the rim. Place another biscuit on top of the ice cream, flat side up, pressing down lightly so it sticks to the ice cream. Gently lift the rings off the sandwiches.

Spread the nuts onto a baking tray and gently roll the sides of each sandwich in the nuts to coat. Serve immediately or freeze until ready to serve.

MELTING MOMENTS
Biscuit Yo-yos
Makes 20

Melting moments are a great afternoon treat that many grandmothers would have in their recipe book. This recipe incorporates a delicious cheesecake filling.

1. PREPARE THE CHEESECAKE FILLING
Make the filling following the recipe for New York Cheesecake (see recipe). Set aside in the refrigerator until the filling is set.

2. PREPARE THE BISCUITS
Remove the plastic wrap and, using a rolling pin, roll the dough between 2 sheets of baking paper to about ¼in (5mm) in thickness. Rest in the refrigerator for 10 minutes. Remove the top sheet and, using a cutter, cut 40 discs—each disc should weigh about ⅙oz (5g) and you will need 2 discs per biscuit. Using a spatula, carefully place the discs on a lined baking tray, allowing a ¾in (2cm) gap between each biscuit.

Preheat the oven to 340°F (170°C/Gas Mark 3). Bake the biscuits for 12–15 minutes. Once baked, remove the biscuits from the baking tray and place on a cooling rack.

3. ASSEMBLE AND SERVE
Once cooled, turn over half the biscuits, flat side up. Place the cheesecake filling into a piping bag with star nozzle and pipe about ⅙oz (5g) filling onto each biscuit. Gently press another biscuit, flat side down, onto the cheesecake filling. Dust with confectioner's sugar and serve immediately.

¼ quantity (7oz/200g) New York Cheesecake filling (see New York Passionfruit Cheesecake)

¼ quantity (7oz/200g) Biscuit Dough (see recipe)

pure confectioner's/icing sugar for dusting

EQUIPMENT
1 cutter, round, 1¾in (4cm) diameter
Baking tray
Baking paper
Rolling pin
Piping bag with star nozzle no. 826
Flexible spatula
Cooling rack

DIAMOND BISCUITS

Diamant

MAKES 40 BISCUITS

These pretty little biscuits should sparkle in the light; however, they may not last long as they are so tasty.

½ quantity (14½oz/420g) Biscuit Dough
   (see recipe)
oz (20g) dried apricots, finely chopped
1oz (30g) currants (or any glace or dried
   fruits), finely chopped
grated zest of 1 orange
3½ oz (100g) superfine/caster sugar
1 egg for egg wash
1oz (30g) mixed nuts, chopped

EQUIPMENT

Chopping board

Serrated knife

Plastic wrap

Baking tray

Baking paper

Pastry brush

Knife for cutting fruit

TIPS AND TRICKS

You can add essences to the dough for a
variation of flavours, including coffee,
vanilla or even rum.

1. PREPARE THE BISCUIT DOUGH

While the dough is soft, mix the fruit, nuts and zest into the dough. Lightly flour the bench. Roll the dough into a 24in (60cm) long stick. Sprinkle the sugar evenly on a baking tray. Lightly brush all sides of the dough with egg wash. Roll the dough stick in the sugar until it is evenly coated then rest the dough in the refrigerator for 20 minutes.

2. ASSEMBLE, BAKE AND SERVE

Using a serrated knife, cut the dough stick into ⅔in (1.2cm) thick biscuits. Place on a baking tray lined with baking paper—space the biscuits slightly apart so they don't touch during baking, as they will spread. Brush lightly with egg wash.

Preheat the oven to 340°F (170°C/Gas Mark 3). Bake for 12–15 minutes. Allow to cool, before storing in an airtight container for 3 days.

ROSE BISCUITS
Rose de biscuit

MAKES 24 BISCUITS

These biscuits are the perfect pantry staple—they are easy to prepare and store well.

¼ quantity (7oz/200g) Biscuit Dough (see recipe), at room temperature

12 glace cherries, cut in half

12 pieces of glace ginger, cut in half (24 halves)

EQUIPMENT

Plastic wrap

Piping bag with star nozzle

Knife

Chopping board

Baking tray

Baking paper

TIPS AND TRICKS

Any glace fruits can be used in this recipe. Don't press the fruit down too much or it will disfigure the shape of the biscuit. You may need to weigh down the baking paper with weights to prevent it lifting during baking.

1. PREPARE THE BISCUIT DOUGH

While the dough is soft, place the dough into a piping bag with a star nozzle. Line a baking tray with baking paper. Hold the piping bag upright at a 90-degree angle and about ½–⅔in (1–1.5cm) above the baking paper. Gently squeeze the bag, moving the nozzle in a circular motion to make a 1¼–1¾in (3–4cm) round. Stop squeezing the piping bag and lift the nozzle away to complete the biscuit—the biscuits should weigh about ½oz (15g) each.

2. ASSEMBLE, BAKE AND SERVE

Top each of the biscuits with half a cherry and half a piece of ginger, pushing them in slightly. Place the biscuits in the refrigerator for 15–20 minutes.

Preheat the oven to 340°F (170°C/Gas Mark 3). Bake for 12–15 minutes until lightly golden. Allow to cool before storing in an airtight container for 5 days.

ALMOND AND PISTACHIO BREAD
Biscuit aux Amandes et Pistaches

MAKES 1 LOAF

So easy to prepare and perfect for a homemade Christmas gift. Wrap the biscuits prettily in clear bags with festive ribbon.

1. PREPARE THE MIXTURE

In an electric mixer with whisk attachment, mix the egg whites and sugar to soft peaks (see Glossary) to make a meringue. Stop the machine and, using a spatula, gradually fold in almonds, pistachio, flour and vanilla essence.

2. BAKE AND SERVE

Preheat the oven to 320°F (160°C/Gas Mark 2–3). Brush the loaf tin with melted butter and line with baking paper. Pour the mixture into the tin and spread evenly. Bake for 20 minutes—the loaf will be ready when a skewer comes out clean. Remove from the tin and allow to cool. Once cool, wrap the loaf in plastic wrap and freeze for 24 hours minimum. Remove from the freezer and while the loaf is still frozen, use a serrated knife to thinly slice the bread into 1/8–1/4in (3–5mm) thickness. Lay the biscuits on a baking tray and bake the biscuits at 340°F (170°C/Gas Mark 3) for 15–20 minutes. Once cooled, store in an airtight container for up to 3 days—unbaked the loaf can be kept in the freezer for up to 1 month.

5oz (150g) egg whites (5 eggs)

3½ oz (100g) superfine/caster sugar

2oz (55g) almonds, unblanched, whole

2oz (55g) pistachios, whole

5½oz (160g) all-purpose/plain flour

1 teaspoon vanilla essence

softened butter, for greasing

EQUIPMENT

Electric mixer with whisk attachment

Flexible spatula

Plastic wrap

Loaf tin, 10in (25cm) x 3¾in (9cm) x 3¼in (8cm)

Serrated knife

Baking paper

Baking tray

Skewer to test

TIPS AND TRICKS

You can add other ingredients such as chopped thyme, rosemary and spices.

Biscuit Dough

SPICED BISCUIT

Speculoos

MAKES 30 BISCUITS

Speculoos biscuits are popular in the North of France and the Netherlands. They are eaten traditionally to celebrate St Nicholas. The name is from the Latin word speculum, which means 'a mirror', as often the biscuits have an image stamped on them.

½ quantity (14½oz/420g) Biscuit Dough
   (see recipe)

⅓oz (10g) mixed spice

5 pinches cinnamon, ground

EQUIPMENT

Cutter, round, 2¾in (7cm) diameter

Rolling pin

Baking tray

Baking paper

TIPS AND TRICKS

To make mixed spice: Combine
4 teaspoons cinnamon, 2 teaspoons ground
coriander, 1 teaspoon allspice, ½ teaspoon
ground nutmeg, ½ teaspoon ground
ginger and ½ teaspoon ground cloves.

1. PREPARE THE BISCUIT DOUGH

Make the dough following the recipe for Biscuit Dough (see recipe). Add the mixed spice and cinnamon and mix into the dough. Roll the dough between 2 sheets of baking paper to a ¼in (5mm) thickness. Allow to rest for 5 minutes in the refrigerator. Remove the top sheet of baking paper and, using a cutter, cut out discs—each biscuit should weigh about ¾oz (25g). Place the biscuits evenly on a baking tray lined with baking paper.

2. ASSEMBLE, BAKE AND SERVE

Preheat the oven to 340°F (170°C/Gas Mark 3). Bake for 12–15 minutes. Allow to cool before storing in an airtight container for 3 days.

LEMON CURD TARTLET
Tartelette au Citron

MAKES 20 MINI TARTLETS

These lemon curd tartlets are always a great favourite and wonderful for serving as an afternoon tea treat or dinner petit fours.

LEMON CURD

Makes 9oz (250g)

⅛oz (3g) gelatine leaves (1 leaf)

2¼fl oz (75ml) pouring cream

2¼fl oz (75ml) lemon juice (about 3 lemons)

grated zest of ½ lemon

2 eggs (1¾–2oz/50–55g each)

2oz (55g) superfine/caster sugar

1oz (30g) unsalted butter, diced and soft

softened butter for greasing

flour for dusting

TART BASE

½ quantity (14½oz/420g) Biscuit Dough
  (see recipe)

1. PREPARE THE TARTLET BASE

Prepare the tart moulds by brushing inside with softened butter, dust with flour and shake off any excess—this will ensure the dough doesn't stick to the tins after baking. Lightly flour a clean surface on your kitchen bench, remove the plastic wrap from the dough and, using a rolling pin, roll the dough to a ¼in (5mm) thickness. Using the cutter, cut 20 circles. Place one circle over the tartlet mould and, starting from the centre, press in the dough lightly with your fingers, working your way around the base and then up the sides. Take the rolling pin and roll over the top of the mould—this will cut the top edges, giving you a clean finish. Repeat with the rest of the dough and moulds. Rest the dough in the refrigerator for 20 minutes.

Preheat the oven to 345°F (175°C/Gas Mark 4). Prepare the tart bases with baking weights (see Before you Begin). Bake the bases for 20 minutes. Allow bases to cool before removing from moulds.

2. PREPARE THE LEMON CURD FILLING

Soak the gelatine leaf, fully submerged, in a bowl of cold water. Place the cream into a saucepan, add the lemon juice and zest, and bring to the boil, which should take about 2 minutes. Meanwhile, whisk the eggs and sugar in another bowl. Once the cream mixture has come to the boil, gradually add it to the egg mixture, continually whisking. Pour the mixture back into the saucepan and whisk over a medium to high heat until it comes to the boil—it will thicken, which should take about 1 minute. Remove the saucepan from the heat and continue to whisk. Squeeze the water out of the gelatine then whisk the gelatine

EQUIPMENT

20 tartlet moulds, 2½in (6cm) diameter x
   ¾in (2cm) deep

Mixing bowls, 8in (20cm) diameter

Plastic wrap

Rolling pin

Baking weights

Cutter, round, 2½ in (6cm) diameter

Grater

Saucepan, 8in (20cm) diameter

Whisk

Hand juicer

Plate

Sieve

Piping bag and no. 804 nozzle

TIPS AND TRICKS

Candied lemon zest—lemon zest in any
shape which has been cooked in a sugar
syrup and is used for decoration.

and diced butter into the lemon curd mixture. Pass the curd
through a sieve (see Glossary) onto a plate. Cover with plastic
wrap, making sure the plastic is in direct contact with the surface
to avoid a skin forming. Refrigerate for at least 1 hour before
using. Lemon curd can be kept in the refrigerator for up to
3 days.

3. ASSEMBLE AND SERVE

Place the prebaked tartlet bases onto a tray or platter. Place the
set lemon curd into a bowl and whisk to a smooth consistency.
Place the curd into a piping bag with nozzle and fill the tartlet
case almost to the rim. Place tarts in the refrigerator to set before
serving.

BISCOTTI

Biscotti originates from a Latin word which means twice cooked or baked. In Italy they are also known as Biscotti di Prato or if you are in Tuscany they are called Cantucinni and enjoyed with a Vin Santo which is a fabulous dessert wine.

1. PREPARE THE MIXTURE

In the bowl of an electric mixer with paddle attachment, place the sugar, flour, baking powder, egg and zest, and mix on low speed until just combined—about 2 minutes. Add the nuts and mix until all combined, another 30 seconds—do not overmix as you don't want to break up the nuts.

2. ASSEMBLE, BAKE AND SERVE

Preheat the oven to 340°F (170°C/Gas Mark 3). Roll the dough into an 8in (20cm) log and bake for 20 minutes. Remove from the oven and set aside to cool for 10 minutes. Reduce the oven to 325°F (160°C/Gas Mark 2–3). Using a serrated knife, cut the log into ½in (1cm) slices on a slight angle—about 14 slices. Place the cut biscuits on their sides on a baking tray lined with baking paper and bake for a further 15–20 minutes. Biscotti can be stored in an airtight container for up to 3 weeks.

3½oz (100g) superfine/caster sugar

3¾oz (110g) all-purpose/plain flour

¹/₆oz (5g) baking powder

1 egg (1¾–2oz/50–55g)

grated zest of ½ orange

1¾oz (50g) hazelnuts, unroasted

EQUIPMENT

Electric mixer with paddle attachment

Serrated knife

Baking paper

Baking tray

Grater

TIPS AND TRICKS

You can add other ingredients such as chopped thyme, rosemary and spices of your choice.

CHOCOLATE & SALTED CARAMEL TART

Tarte au Chocolat et Caramel au Beurre Salé

MAKES 4 INDIVIDUAL TARTS

This dessert was featured on MasterChef—Salted Caramel is such an amazing combination we just can't get enough of it.

I. PREPARE THE CHOCOLATE SABLE DOUGH

Place flour, almond meal, cocoa powder and cold butter into a mixing bowl and rub the ingredients between your hands until it forms a sandy texture—this should take minutes. Add the salt, baking powder, sugar and whole egg, then mix with one hand to make a firm dough. Do this for 2 minutes until all combined. Wrap the dough in plastic wrap and refrigerate for at least 20 minutes before using.

Prepare the tart moulds by brushing inside with softened butter, dust with flour and shake off any excess. Lightly flour a clean surface, remove the plastic wrap from the dough and, using a rolling pin, roll the dough to a ¼in (5mm) thickness. Cut out 4 circles of dough using a round cutter with a 5in (13cm) diameter. Place a circle over a tart mould and press in the dough lightly with your fingers, from the centre, around the base and then up the sides. Take the rolling pin and roll over the top of the mould. Repeat with the rest of the dough and moulds. Rest the dough in the refrigerator for 20 minutes. Preheat the oven to 345°F (175°C/Gas Mark 4). Prepare the tart bases with baking weights (see Before you Begin). Bake for about 10–15 minutes.

2. PREPARE THE SALTED CARAMEL FILLING

Place the sugar and glucose into a larger saucepan and pour the cream into a smaller saucepan. Place the cream in a smaller saucepan and place over a high heat and bring to the boil, then remove from stovetop and set aside. Place the glucose and then sugar into the larger saucepan and place on a medium to high heat and stir with a wooden spoon until it reaches a honey brown colour then remove from the stove. Continuously whisk the caramel while slowly adding in the cream until all lumps have disappeared—be careful

CHOCOLATE SABLE DOUGH

Makes 14½oz (420g)

6oz (175g) all-purpose/plain flour

⅙oz (5g) almond meal

½oz (15g) Dutch cocoa powder

3¾oz (110g) unsalted butter, ⅔in (1.5cm) cubes, cold

2 pinches table salt

⅛oz (4g) baking powder

2½ oz (75g) pure confectioner's/icing sugar, sifted

1 egg (1¾–2oz/50–55g)

softened butter for greasing

flour for dusting

SALTED CARAMEL

Makes 7oz (200g)

3¾oz (115g) superfine/caster sugar

1½oz (45g) liquid glucose

2¾fl oz (100ml) pouring cream

⅕ oz (5g) salt

oz (20g) unsalted butter, chopped, room temperature

Biscuit Dough

CHOCOLATE GANACHE

Makes 11½oz (330g)

5½fl oz (160ml) pouring cream

1¾oz (50g) milk chocolate, chopped

3½ oz (100g) dark chocolate, chopped

oz (20g) unsalted butter

NOUGATINE

Makes 7oz (200g)

1¾oz (50g) liquid glucose

3½ oz (100g) superfine/caster sugar

1/6oz (5g) table salt

1fl oz (30ml) water

2½oz (80g) roasted nuts

EQUIPMENT

Mixing bowl, 8in (20cm)

Knife

Chopping board

Round cutter, 5in (13cm) diameter

4 tart moulds, 4in (10cm) x 1in (2.5cm),
  fluted

Plastic wrap

3 saucepans, 8in (20cm) diameter

Saucepan, 6in (15cm) diameter

Wooden spoon

Whisk

Flexible spatula

Wooden spoon

Baking paper

Baking tray

Rolling pin

Baking weights

as the cream will bubble furiously and the steam is very hot, so add gradually otherwise it may overflow. Add the salt and butter, and whisk until all is combined then set aside to cool. The caramel can be kept at room temperature in an airtight container for up to 3 days.

3. PREPARE THE CHOCOLATE GANACHE

Place the cream in a saucepan over a medium to high heat, and bring to the boil. Remove the pan from heat, add both chocolates and stir well with a whisk. Add the butter and continue stirring until all is well combined. The ganache can be stored in a refrigerator for up to 3 days.

4. PREPARE THE NOUGATINE

Place the glucose, sugar, salt and water into a saucepan, and cook over a medium to high heat, stirring with a wooden spoon, until the mixture reaches a light honey colour. Remove the pan from the heat and stir in the nuts. Once nuts are well combined, pour onto an baking tray lined with baking paper. Set aside to cool at room temperature then chop to desired size. Nougatine can be kept in an airtight container for up to 3 days.

5. ASSEMBLE AND SERVE

Arrange the prebaked tart shells on a tray or platter that will fit into your refrigerator. Pour about ⅔oz (20g) of liquid salted caramel into the moulds and set in the refrigerator for 10 minutes. Then pour the chocolate ganache over the top of the set salted caramel to the rim of the pastry and chill again for 5 minutes. Remove from the refrigerator and decorate with pieces of nougatine (about ¼oz/7g per tart). Serve at room temperature so that the caramel is liquid when eaten.

TIPS AND TRICKS

Measure the glucose into the saucepan using a wet spoon to stop the glucose from sticking.

For the salted caramel, use a small saucepan or pot—this will help reduce the steam that could result and you have less chance of burning yourself.

Use a whisk with a long handle.

To bring the salted caramel and ganache back to pouring consistency, gently reheat while stirring continuously. This can only be done once.

To make great ganache, always use couverture chocolate and when adding butter make sure it is combined properly.

BAKED CHOCOLATE TART
Tarte au Chocolat

LARGE
SERVES 6 TO 8

A delicious tart that will be a crowd pleaser and so easy to prepare.

TART BASE

softened butter for greasing

flour for dusting

1 quantity (30oz/840g) Biscuit Dough (see
   recipe)

CHOCOLATE FILLING

6fl oz (180ml) pouring cream

4fl oz (120ml) milk

10½oz (300g) dark chocolate (70% cocoa),
   chopped

2 eggs (1¾–2oz/50–55g each), lightly beaten

EQUIPMENT

Mixing bowl, 8in (20cm)

Knife

Plastic wrap

Tart mould, 8in (20cm) x 1½in (4cm)

Rolling pin

Baking weights

Saucepan, 6in (15cm)

1. PREPARE THE TART BASE

Prepare the tart mould by brushing inside with softened butter, dust with flour and shake off any excess—this will ensure the dough doesn't stick to the mould after baking. Lightly flour a clean surface on your kitchen bench, remove the plastic wrap from the dough and, using a rolling pin, roll the dough to a ¼in (5mm) thickness. Using a rolling pin, gently wrap the dough around the rolling pin, then slowly unwind the dough over the mould. Starting from the centre, press in the dough lightly with your fingers, working your way around the base and then up the sides. Take the rolling pin and roll over the top of the mould—this will cut the top edges, giving you a clean finish. Rest the dough in the refrigerator for 20 minutes.

Preheat the oven to 340°F (170°C/Gas Mark 3). Prepare the tart base with baking weights (see Before you Begin). Bake for about 10–15 minutes. Allow to cool.

2. PREPARE THE CHOCOLATE FILLING

In a saucepan, bring the cream and milk to the boil then add the chopped chocolate. Slowly add the beaten eggs and continue mixing until smooth.

3. ASSEMBLE, BAKE AND SERVE

Pour the chocolate filling into the prebaked tart base. Bake in the oven at 200°F (100°C/Gas Mark ½) for 25–30 minutes. Remove when the centre is still wobbly and place in the refrigerator to set for 1 hour. Serve chilled or at room temperature.

Puff Pastry
Pâte Feuilletée

PUFF PASTRY

Pâte Feuilletée

MAKES 24OZ (675G)

Pâte feuilletée is a rich and delicate pastry made of very thin layers with its origins dating back to the seventeenth century. When making this dough, give yourself plenty of time as the rolling and folding process is repeated a number of times. Always rest this dough in the refrigerator overnight before use.

9oz (250g) all-purpose/plain flour

1/6oz (6g) table salt

¾oz (25g) unsalted butter, softened, room temperature

4½fl oz (130ml) cold water

7oz (200g) unsalted butter, softened, room temperature, for folding

EQUIPMENT

Electric mixer with hook attachment

Rolling pin

Plastic wrap

Baking paper

Baking tray

1. In the bowl of an electric mixer with a hook attachment, place the flour, salt and ¾oz (25g) butter, and add cold water.

2. Mix on low speed until a dough starts to form, then increase to medium and let it turn for 3 minutes. Remove the dough from the bowl and place on a lightly floured bench top. Using a rolling pin, roll the dough into a 9in (22cm) square and wrap in plastic wrap. Place the dough in the refrigerator to rest for 1 hour.

3. Take the 7oz (200g) butter and place between 2 pieces of baking paper. Push it down to a 5in (12cm) square and set it aside. Once the dough has been rested, place as a diamond shape on a lightly floured bench top. Roll the four corners out as though you want to roll a cross shape, then place the butter in the centre. Fold the four sides into the centre of the cross so that it becomes a square—seal and pinch the creases tightly otherwise the butter will leak when rolling. Using a rolling pin, roll the dough to a rectangle 19–20in (48–50cm) long, then turn the dough 90 degrees so that its longer side runs parallel to the edge of the table, and fold the dough into thirds—this represents one folding step. Allow to rest in the refrigerator for 30 minutes and then repeat the folding step. Rest in the refrigerator for 24 hours before continuing.

4. After 24 hours, place the dough on a lightly floured bench top and repeat the folding step process three more times with at least 30 minutes resting in the refrigerator between turns. At this stage the dough has been through the folding step five times, which is the basic requirement of successful puff pastry dough. Once completed, place in the refrigerator to rest for 20 minute before using. This dough can be stored in the refrigerator for up to 3 days or in the freezer for 1 month.

TIPS AND TRICKS
Do not be put off by the time required to make this dough—it's the 'rock star' of pastry doughs and so versatile.
Never rush this recipe as it needs to be rested properly.
You can add 1 teaspoon of white vinegar into the water to help preserve the dough.

ROUGH PUFF

Pâte Feuilletée Rapide

MAKES 24 OZ (675G)

This alternative to puff pastry is easier and quicker to produce as there is less labour involved. The finished product will be similar to puff pastry; however, it will not be as light and flaky.

9oz (250g) all-purpose/plain flour

9oz (250g) unsalted butter, cold and diced

1/8oz (4g) table salt

4fl oz (125ml) water, ice cold

EQUIPMENT

Food processor

Rolling pin

Plastic wrap

1. In a food processor, pulse flour, butter and salt until combined and pour in the cold water—continue pulsing until a dough has been formed.

2. Remove from the food processor and place on a lightly floured bench top. Using a rolling pin, roll the dough into a 9in (22cm) square and wrap in plastic wrap. Place the dough in the refrigerator to rest for 1 hour.

3. Using a rolling pin, roll the dough to a rectangle 19–20in (48–50cm) long, then turn the dough 90 degrees so that it's longer side runs parallel to the edge of the table, and fold the dough into thirds—this represents one folding step. Allow to rest in the refrigerator for 10 minutes and then repeat the folding step four times—resting in the refrigerator for 10 minutes between each turn. Finally, rest in the refrigerator for 1 hour before using. This dough can be stored in the refrigerator for up to 3 days or in the freezer for 1 month.

VANILLA SLICE

Millefeuille

MAKES 5 INDIVIDUAL

Millefeuille translated means a thousand leaves and this dessert is layers of puff pastry filled with crème pâtissière—pastry's most versatile and used filling. This recipe can be created and flavoured so many different ways and is so light and delicate to eat.

1. PREPARE THE CRÈME PÂTISSIÈRE

Place the milk and the scraped vanilla bean into a saucepan and bring to the boil over medium heat. In a mixing bowl, whisk the egg yolks with the sugar and whisk until all the sugar is dissolved. Add the flour and cornstarch, and whisk until a paste has formed. When the milk is at boiling point, gradually stir it into the egg mixture. Mix thoroughly and place the mixture back into the saucepan over medium heat and whisk vigorously. The mixture will thicken and eventually bubbles will appear—keep cooking the mixture for a further 1 minute which allows the flours to cook out. Place the mixture onto a plate and place a piece of plastic wrap on the top—this ensures a skin does not form on the crème pâtissière. Chill in the refrigerator for about 20 minutes.

To use the crème pâtissière after it has been chilled, place it into a bowl then whisk the mixture to smooth the consistency. You may wish to add whipped cream as this will make the crème pâtissière lighter in terms of taste and texture.

2. PREPARE THE PUFF PASTRY

Preheat the oven to 345°F (175°C/Gas Mark 4). Line a standard baking tray, 16in x 12in (40cm x 30cm), with baking paper. Roll out the dough to the size of the tray. Place ¾in- (2cm) high ovenproof weights in each corner around the puff and place a cooling rack on top. This will prevent the puff pastry from rising too high and to allow it to keep a defined shape. Bake for 25 minutes, then reduce the oven to 340°F (170°C/Gas Mark 3) and bake for a further 15–20 minutes. This will allow the puff pastry to dry and results in a flaky dough. Once cooked remove from oven

CRÈME PÂTISSIÈRE

Makes 10½oz (300g)

16fl oz (500ml) milk

1 vanilla bean, scraped (see Glossary)

4 egg yolks

2oz (60g) superfine/caster sugar

⅔oz (20g) all-purpose/plain flour

⅔oz (20g) cornstarch/cornflour

5½oz (160g) whipped cream, optional

1 quantity (24oz/675g) Puff Pastry Dough (see recipe)

pure confectioner's/icing sugar for dusting

Puff Pastry

and leave the pastry to cool for about 20 minutes. Place the puff pastry on top of a chopping board and, using a serrated knife, cut the edges to obtain 4 clean sides.

3. ASSEMBLE AND SERVE

Take the pastry and cut evenly into 16 pieces. Three squares will make one portion of millefeuille so, out of 16 squares, you will get 5 portions (3 x 5) with one spare. Line the portions side by side so that you have 5 rows of 3. Place the crème pâtissière into a piping bag with nozzle and, starting with the bottom row, pipe the crème pâtissière onto each piece—there should be about $^{2}/_{3}$oz (20g) of crème pâtissière per piece. Pipe from the outside of the square to the centre, following the natural line of the pastry, and continue until the entire bottom row is completed. Place the middle row of puff pastry pieces onto the piped crème pâtissière pieces—you should now have a rectangle of pastry, crème pâtissière and pastry. Repeat layering of crème pâtissière and puff pastry. The end result should be 3 layers of puff pastry and 2 layers of crème pâtissière in between. Dust with confectioner's sugar and serve immediately.

EQUIPMENT

Saucepan, 8in (20cm) diameter

Whisk

Flexible spatula

Mixing bowl, 8in (20cm) diameter

Plate

Plastic wrap

2 baking trays

Chopping board

24 tartlet moulds, 2½in (6cm) x ¾in (2cm) deep

Baking paper

Cooling rack

Serrated knife

Piping bag and no. 804 nozzle

TIPS AND TRICKS

Three-quarter inch (2cm) ovenproof weights can be stacked tartlet moulds or small ceramic moulds—anything ovenproof that holds the cooling rack ¾in (2cm) above the puff pastry. To make a large millefeuille, cut the sheet of puff pastry into thirds and follow layering steps—allow to set in the refrigerator for 10 minutes before cutting and serving. You can add seasonal fruit by placing it on the puff pastry layer before piping on the crème pâtissière—for example, use the poached pear (see Pear Bourdaloue) or apple compote (see Caramelised Apple Tart).

Puff Pastry

GALETTE
Galette à la Crème d'Amande
MAKES 4

This delightful pastry is composed of almond cream inside two puff pastry discs.

ALMOND CREAM

¾oz (25g) unsalted butter, softened

1oz (30g) superfine/caster sugar

1 egg (1¾–2oz/50–55g)

1½oz (40g) ground almonds

1/6oz (5g) all-purpose/plain flour

1 teaspoon dark rum

1 quantity (24oz/675g) Puff Pastry Dough
  (see recipe)

1 egg for egg wash

1¾oz (50g) honey

EQUIPMENT

Mixing bowls, 8in (20cm) diameter

Whisk

Rolling pin

Cutter, 3¾in (9cm), fluted

Cutter, 4in (10cm), fluted

Pastry brush

Baking tray

Baking paper

TIPS AND TRICKS

To lighten the almond cream, place a small amount of crème pâtissière in the mix and it becomes frangipane.
Add a few drops of almond essence to enhance the flavour.

1. PREPARE THE ALMOND CREAM

In a mixing bowl, whisk the butter and sugar until all the sugar has been incorporated into the butter and it lightens in colour. Add the egg, ground almond, flour and rum, and mix until all combined.

2. PREPARE THE PUFF PASTRY

Lightly flour a clean benchtop. Cut the puff pastry dough in half then roll each into an 8in (20cm) x 16in (40cm) rectangular shape, 1/6in (4mm) thick. From one piece, cut eight 3¾in (9cm) discs using a cutter and place on a baking tray lined with baking paper. From the remaining puff pastry piece, cut eight 4in (10cm) discs using a cutter then set aside. Take the eight 3¾in (9cm) discs and place 1 tablespoon almond cream (about 1½oz/40g) into the centre of each disc then brush lightly all around the almond cream with egg wash. Place the larger discs (4in/10cm) on top and press all around the edges to seal the layers—you may need to trim the edges with the 3¾in (9cm) cutter to create a more even edge. Place in the refrigerator to rest for 20 minutes.

3. ASSEMBLE, BAKE AND SERVE

Preheat the oven to 345°F (175°C/Gas Mark 4). Remove the unbaked galettes and brush them again with egg wash then place on a baking tray lined with baking paper. Bake for about 30 minutes until golden and crispy. After baking, drizzle honey on the top of the galettes to give a glossy finish. The galettes are best eaten within 4 hours of baking. They can be frozen, unbaked, for up to 1 month—remove from the freezer at least 10 minutes prior to baking.

PALM PASTRY
Palmier

MAKES 12

Palmier is a French word for 'palm tree'—these delights are made of sugar and double-rolled puff pastry to resemble the distinctive shape of palm leaves.

1 quantity (24oz/675g) Puff Pastry Dough
  (see recipe)
1 egg for egg wash
3½ oz (100g) superfine/caster sugar

EQUIPMENT
Rolling pin
Pastry brush
Baking tray
Baking paper
Knife

TIPS AND TRICKS
Different flavours can be added to a palmier, such as cinnamon. You can even create a savoury flavour, such as Parmesan replacing the sugar.
Refrigerating before cutting makes the palmier easier to slice.

1. PREPARE THE PUFF PASTRY

Cut the puff pastry dough into half then roll each half into an 8in (20cm) x 16in (40cm) rectangular shape, ⅙in (4mm) thick. Brush a small amount of egg wash over the top then evenly sprinkle with the sugar. Fold the pastry from the two ends, 1in (3cm) in from the edge, and keep folding each side until you meet at the centre.

Lightly brush egg wash all over the pastry and sprinkle with more sugar, then cut 12 pieces each ⅔in (1.5cm) thick—weighing about ¾oz (25g) each. Line a baking tray with baking paper and place the palmiers 2in (5cm) apart, as they will expand during cooking. Sprinkle with a little more sugar.

2. BAKE AND SERVE

Preheat the oven to 345°F (175°C/Gas Mark 4). Bake for 12–15 minutes until golden. Remove from the oven and rest for 10 minutes before serving—they are best eaten immediately. The palmiers can be frozen, unbaked, for up to 1 month.

MATCH BISCUITS
Biscuit Allumettes

MAKES 10 BISCUITS

*Biscuit allumettes are perfect for puff pastry addicts as the only addition is sugar.
They are also ideal served with coffee or tea.*

½ quantity (11½oz/340g) Puff Pastry Dough
   (see recipe)

1 egg for egg wash

2½oz (80g) superfine/caster sugar or raw sugar

EQUIPMENT

Rolling pin

Baking tray

Baking paper

Pastry brush

Knife

1. PREPARE THE PUFF PASTRY

Roll the dough into a 14in (35cm) x 10in (25cm) rectangle, about
⅙in (4mm) thickness. Lightly egg wash the entire sheet and
sprinkle the sugar evenly on top. Roll the rolling pin over the
top to secure the sugar to the dough. Cut the dough lengthways
then cut into 10 strips of 1¾in (4cm) x 3¼in (8cm).

2. BAKE AND SERVE

Preheat the oven to 340°F (170°C/Gas Mark 3). Line a baking tray
with baking paper and place the puff pastry pieces evenly spaced
apart on the tray. Bake for 15 minutes. Remove and set aside to
cool. Best eaten straight away, served at room temperature. The
biscuits can be frozen, unbaked, for up to 1 month.

CARAMELISED APPLE TART
Tarte Tatin

INDIVIDUAL
MAKES 4 INDIVIDUAL

Fanny and Caroline Tatin ran a restaurant in the Hotel Tatin in Lamotte-Beuvron in France—a cooking disaster ended up a cooking masterpiece and they became true creators of the famous tarte tatin.

½ quantity (11½oz/340g) Puff Pastry Dough
   (see recipe)

2½oz (80g) superfine/caster sugar

4 Granny Smith apples, small to medium

2/3oz (20g) unsalted butter, melted

1 teaspoon vanilla essence

1. PREPARE THE PUFF PASTRY DOUGH

Roll the dough into a 14in (35cm) x 10in (25cm) rectangle, about ⅙in (4mm) thickness. Roll the dough sheet onto the rolling pin and transfer to a tray that will fit into your refrigerator and allow to rest for 20 minutes.

Place a piece of A4 size silicon paper onto the bench top. Take a 4in (10cm) round mould and draw around the base to create an outline, then cut around the line with scissors. Place into a lightly buttered mould. Repeat for each mould.

2. PREPARE A DRY CARAMEL

Sprinkle the sugar to cover the bottom of a small frying pan and place over medium heat on the stovetop. Stir continually with a wooden spoon—the sugar will start to melt and eventually caramelise (see Glossary). Bring the caramel to a dark honey colour then pour the hot liquid evenly into the four moulds, making sure the bottom of each mould is covered. Set aside and allow to cool.

3. PREPARING THE APPLES

Preheat the oven to 350°F (180°C/Gas Mark 4).

Peel and core the apples then cut each into 8 segments. Put the apple wedges into a large bowl, add the melted butter and vanilla essence. Toss the wedges around so they are coated well. Arrange the apple wedges into each mould on top of the caramel—8 wedges per mould.

EQUIPMENT

4 tart moulds, 4in (10cm) diameter x 1in (2.5cm) high, fluted

Frying pan, 8in (20cm)

Mixing bowl, 8in (20cm)

Rolling pin

Wooden spoon

Silicon paper, A4 size

Cutter, 5½in (13cm), round

Baking tray

Baking paper

Scissors

Pencil/pen

Peeler

Apple corer

Knife

4. ASSEMBLE, BAKE AND SERVE

Take the rolled puff pastry from the refrigerator and place it on your kitchen bench. Cut the pastry into four discs, each 5½in (13cm) diameter. Place the discs on top of the apple wedges, pressing lightly to seal the puff pastry to the apple. Bake at 350°F (180°C/Gas Mark 4) for 18–20 minutes until golden brown and crunchy. Remove from the oven and rest for 5 minutes with a baking tray on top to create weight.

Remove the baking tray after 5 minutes. Turn the tart upside down onto an individual plate—the puff pastry on the bottom, apple on the top. Serve warm with a good quality vanilla ice cream.

CHEESESTICKS
Bâtonnets au Fromage

MAKES 10 BISCUITS

These biscuits are absolutely delicious and perfect any time—teatime, snacks or with drinks. They can even be used to add crunchiness to savoury dishes.

1. PREPARE THE PUFF PASTRY DOUGH

Preheat the oven to 350°F (180°C/Gas Mark 4) full fan. Lightly flour the kitchen bench. Using a rolling pin, roll the dough into a 14in (35cm) x 10in (25cm) rectangle, about ⅙in (4mm) thick. Lightly brush the dough with egg wash then sprinkle cheese to cover the dough. Season with pepper and salt to taste. Cut into ten 1¾in (4cm) long strips. Hold each end of one strip and twist in opposite directions until fully enclosed.

2. BAKE AND SERVE

Line a baking tray with baking paper and lay out each pastry strip. Bake for 15–18 minutes. Serve immediately, warm or at room temperature. The unbaked dough can be frozen for up to 1 month and then baked as required; it may need an extra 10 minutes baking time from frozen.

2½oz (80g) cheddar cheese, grated

black pepper to taste

salt to taste

1 egg for egg wash

½ quantity (11½oz/340g) Puff Pastry Dough (see recipe)

EQUIPMENT

Rolling pin

Pastry brush

Baking tray

Baking paper

Knife

PORTUGUESE TART VINCENT'S WAY
Pastel de Nata

MAKES 12

This custard tart was said to have been created by Catholic Monks in the 18th century at a monastery in Santa Maria del Belém. It's also a great way to use leftover puff pastry.

1. PREPARE THE PUFF PASTRY DOUGH

Lightly flour a bench top. Lightly butter and flour the mould. Roll the dough into an 8in (20cm) x 16in (40cm) rectangle, ⅙in (4mm) thick. Cut 8 discs using the cutter. Place a disc into each muffin mould, pressing down so the dough is set neatly in the mould then dock each base (see Glossary).

2. ASSEMBLE, BAKE AND SERVE

Preheat oven to 345°F (175°C/Gas Mark 4) full fan. Spoon the crème pâtissière into each of the moulds lined with pastry—about 2oz (60g) mixture each. Bake for 18 minutes. Remove from the oven and rest the tarts for 20 minutes before unmoulding. Dust sugar on the top, then serve immediately.

1½ quantities 16½oz (480g) Crème Pâtissière
(see Vanilla Slice)

½ quantity (11½oz/340g) Puff Pastry Dough
(see recipe)

softened butter for greasing

flour for dusting

3½ oz (100g) confectioner's/icing sugar

EQUIPMENT

Muffin mould, 12 holes, 3in (7.5cm) x 1¾in
(4cm) height

Cutter, round 4in (10cm) diameter

Spoon

Rolling pin

APPLE TURNOVER
Chausson aux Pommes

MAKES 8

In French, chausson is a children's shoe—this recipe is a classic found all over France.

APPLE COMPOTE

Makes 11oz (320g)

1 quantity (24oz/675g) Puff Pastry Dough
  (see recipe)

4 Granny Smith apples, medium

1¾oz (50g) superfine/caster sugar

2 teaspoons vanilla essence

5 pinches ground cinnamon

7fl oz (200ml) water

2/3fl oz (20ml) Calvados

1 egg for egg wash

1¾oz (50g) honey

EQUIPMENT

Rolling pin

Mixing bowls, 8in (20cm)

Saucepan, 8in (20cm) diameter

Wooden spoon

Plate

Plastic wrap

Cutter, 5½in (13cm) diameter (or a bowl)

Small knife

Peeler

Apple corer

Baking tray

Baking paper

Pastry brush

1. PREPARE THE PUFF PASTRY DOUGH

Lightly flour a bench top. Using a rolling pin, roll the dough to 16in (40cm) x 12in (30cm) rectangle, about ⅛in (3mm) thickness, then cut into 8 discs. Roll each disc, from the centre, to form an 8in (20cm) oval.

2. PREPARE THE APPLE COMPOTE

Peel and core the apples then cut into half; cut each half into 4 wedges then 4 again—you should have 16 cubes of apple. Place the sugar into a mixing bowl with the apple, vanilla essence and cinnamon then mix well. Transfer to a saucepan and add the water and calvados. Cook over a medium heat and keep stirring until no liquid appears at the bottom of the pan—the apples should be half broken down. Transfer to a plate and cover with plastic wrap to avoid a skin forming. This compote will keep for 3 days in the refrigerator—it cannot be frozen.

3. ASSEMBLE, BAKE AND SERVE

Preheat the oven to 345°F (175°C/Gas Mark 4). Line a baking tray with baking paper. Score (see Glossary) half of each dough oval with the back of a knife, flip over and lightly egg wash the edge. Place the compote—about 2oz (60g)—on top of the non-scored side. Fold the other half of the pastry on top and press down with your fingers to seal. Repeat for remaining turnovers. These can be stored in the refrigerator before baking for 1 day or can be frozen, unbaked, for up to 1 month.

Place the turnovers on the baking tray, allowing space between each, and egg wash the tops. Bake for 30 minutes until golden and crunchy. Remove from the oven and glaze the top lightly with a drizzle of honey to give some sparkle. Serve immediately.

FINE APRICOT TART
Tarte Fine à la Abricot

MAKES 2 TARTS, EACH SERVING 6

This is a versatile recipe and any fruit can be substituted, such as mango, berries, rhubarb compote or even banana.

1. PREPARE THE PUFF PASTRY DOUGH

Lightly flour a benchtop. Using a rolling pin, roll the dough to a 16in (40cm) x 11½in (28cm) rectangle, about ⅛in (3mm) thick. Using a 7in (18cm) bowl, press down to cut 2 discs. Line a baking tray with baking paper and place the discs on the tray.

2. ASSEMBLE, BAKE AND SERVE

Preheat the oven to 340°F (170°C/Gas Mark 3). Place the almond cream mix in the centre of each disc and spread thinly until it reaches ½in (1cm) from the edge of the tart. Place the apricots on the cream but not right to the edge, and then sprinkle sugar over each. Bake for 12 minutes then slide off the baking paper and onto the baking rack, and bake for a further 8 minutes. Serve immediate with good quality vanilla icecream.

½ quantity (11½oz/340g) Puff Pastry Dough (see recipe)

⅔oz (20g) Almond Cream (see Galette recipe)

20 apricots, fresh and ripe, cut in half

1¾oz (50g) superfine/caster sugar

EQUIPMENT

Cutter, 7in (18cm) diameter (a bowl can be used)

Rolling pin

Baking tray

Baking rack

Baking paper

Knife

Cutting board

TIPS AND TRICKS

If you are using tinned fruit, about 3½–4oz (100–120g) is required; remember to drain the fruit as you don't want too much liquid to soak the dough. Any fresh stone fruit in season can be substituted for the apricot.

FRUIT HORN
Corne d'Abondance

MAKES 6

An old-fashioned classic pastry where the horn shape is made by winding overlapping pastry strips around a conical mould.

½ quantity (11½oz/340g) Puff Pastry Dough
   (see recipe)

softened butter for greasing

flour for dusting

1 egg for egg wash

1¾oz (50g) superfine/caster sugar

½ quantity (5oz/140g) Crème Pâtissière (see
   Vanilla Slice)

7oz (200g) mixed berries

EQUIPMENT

Metal fruit horn mould, 5½in (13cm) high x
   2in (4.5cm) diameter cone

Pastry brush

Rolling pin

Spoons

TIPS AND TRICKS

You can use a mixture of one part crème chantilly and two parts Crème Pâtissière as the filling. To make crème chantilly, just mix confectioner's/icing sugar with whipped cream and vanilla to taste.

1. PREPARE THE PUFF PASTRY DOUGH

Lightly flour a bench top. Using a rolling pin, roll the dough to a 24in (60cm) x 7in (18cm) rectangle, then cut into 6 strips of 1¼in (3cm) width. Butter and flour the outside of a metal fruit horn mould. Starting from the tip, gently curl the pastry strip around the mould, overlapping ¼–⅓in (5–8mm) until you reach the bottom of the cone. Remember to leave a small tab of pastry hanging over the edge, which can then be folded up on the inside of the mould to secure the shape. Lightly eggwash the pastry and sprinkle with sugar.

2. ASSEMBLE, BAKE AND SERVE

Preheat the oven to 345°F (175°C/Gas Mark 4). Bake for 16–20 minutes. Cool then remove the metal mould. Fill the cone with crème pâtissière and then top with mixed berries. Serve immediately.

PUFF CUBES OF BÉCHAMEL
Carré de Béchamel

MAKES 16

These great little cheese treats are perfect served with wine before a dinner party.

1 quantity (24oz/675g) Puff Pastry Dough
   (see recipe)
flour for dusting

BÉCHAMEL SAUCE
Makes 9oz (250g)
½oz (15g) unsalted butter
1¼oz (35g) all-purpose/plain flour
5fl oz (150ml) milk
1¼oz (35g) goat's cheese
¹/₈oz (4g) blue cheese
1 egg yolk
2 pinches salt
1 pinch pepper

EQUIPMENT
6 moulds for baking, 2½in (6cm) diameter x
   ¾in (2cm) high
Rolling pin
Knife
Cooking rack
Saucepan, 6in (15cm)
Whisk
Baking tray
Baking paper
Piping bag and no. 804 nozzle
Wooden stick (pencil thickness)

1. PREPARE THE PUFF PASTRY DOUGH
Lightly flour the benchtop. Preheat the oven to 345°F (175°C/Gas Mark 4). Line a standard baking tray, 16in (40cm) x 12in (30cm), with baking paper and roll out the dough to the size of the tray. Cut the dough into 16 1¾in (4cm) squares and place squares on baking tray ¾in (2cm) apart. Place ¾in (2cm) high ovenproof weights in each corner around the puff and place a cooling rack on top—this allows the puff pastry to not rise too high.

Bake the puff pastry for 20 minutes, then reduce oven to 340°F (170°C/Gas Mark 3) and bake for a further 10–15 minutes. Remove from the oven and leave the pastry to cool for about 20 minutes. Place the puff pastry on a chopping board and cut the edges with a serrated knife, to obtain 4 clean sides.

2. MAKE THE BÉCHAMEL SAUCE
Melt the butter in a saucepan over medium heat and boil until it reaches a golden brown colour. Add all the flour and whisk for 1 minute to cook out the flour—the mixture should look like a crumble. Take the saucepan off the stove and pour in half the milk while whisking. Once the mixture is smooth, remove from heat and whisk in the rest of the milk, cheese, egg yolk and seasonings. Store in a container with plastic wrap directly in contact with the surface in the refrigerator for up to 3 days—it cannot be frozen.

3. ASSEMBLE AND SERVE
Use a wooden stick to push through one side of the pastry and make a cavity to the centre. Place the béchamel into a piping bag with nozzle, and pipe about ¹/₃oz (10g) béchamel mix per square. Reheat at 340°F (170°C/Gas Mark 3) for 8 minutes. Serve immediately.

Croissant Dough

Pâte à Croissant

CROISSANT DOUGH
Pâte à Croissant

MAKES 8 (2½OZ/80G EACH)

This popular pastry originated in Budapest in 1686 when Turkish soldiers invaded the city at night. The town bakers gave the alert to the city and the invaders were repelled. To celebrate, the bakers created this crescent-shaped pastry—a symbol of the Turkish flag.

Makes 23oz (640g)

9oz (250g) bakers flour

1¾oz (50g) superfine/caster sugar

¾oz (25g) unsalted butter, soft

1/6oz (6g) table salt

2fl oz (65ml) water, tap and hot

2fl oz (65ml) milk, cold

1oz (30g) fresh yeast or 1/3oz (10g) dry yeast

3½oz (100g) unsalted butter, softened (for turning)

1 egg for egg wash

EQUIPMENT

Electric mixer and hook attachment

Rolling pin

Baking tray

Baking paper

Knife

Pastry brush

Plastic wrap

Mixing bowls, 8in (20cm) diameter

Whisk

1. Place the flour, sugar, ¾oz (25g) butter and salt into the bowl of an electric mixer set with the hook attachment. In a separate bowl, mix the hot water and cold milk together, them whisk in the fresh yeast to dissolve it. Add this liquid to the first mixture. Mix on low speed then increase to medium—let it turn for 5 minutes. Remove the dough from the mixer and place on a lightly floured bench. Use your fists to flatten out the dough to a square of about 9in (22cm) and transfer to a baking tray that will fit in your refrigerator. Cover with plastic wrap and allow to rest and rise in the refrigerator for at least 3 hours—ideally overnight.

Meanwhile, take the 3½oz (100g) butter and put between 2 pieces of baking paper then flatten it out with your hands to a square of 5in (12cm); set it aside (the butter can stay at room temperature overnight).

2. Once the dough is rested and ready to use, flour the bench top then start rolling the corners out to resemble a cross shape. Place the softened butter in the centre of the cross. Fold the four sides into the centre of the cross so that it becomes a square—seal and pinch the creases tightly otherwise the butter will leak when rolling.

Roll the dough until it is 19in (48cm) long and then turn the dough 90 degrees. Fold the dough in thirds—this is a single turn—you should get a square of about 6–8in (15–20cm). Roll once again to 19in (48cm) long, then turn the dough to 90 degrees so that its longer side runs parallel to the edge of the table and fold in thirds. At this stage the dough has had 2 single turns. Allow the dough to rest for at least 1 hour in the refrigerator (or preferably overnight).

Unbaked croissants can be frozen—when making the recipe for freezing, add an extra ¹/₃oz (10g) yeast, as yeast will lose some strength when frozen.

Fresh yeast is available at most speciality food stores. If you cannot source fresh yeast, substitute dry yeast—just dilute in the mix of hot water and cold milk before adding the other ingredients.

Remove from the refrigerator and place the dough on a lightly floured surface and roll to 19in (48cm) long then fold in thirds (this is the third turn). Rest in the refrigerator for 1 hour before use.

Remove the dough from the refrigerator, roll it into a 15in (38cm) x 12in (30cm) rectangle, then turn the dough 90 degrees. Cut a triangle shape approximately 3¼in (8cm) x 1¼in (3cm) long. Repeat with the rest of the pastry.

Place the triangles the same way in a row in font of you and start rolling from the 1¼in (3cm) base until you reach the tip. Put the rolled croissant onto a baking tray lined with baking paper and cover lightly with plastic wrap—do not make it too tight as this will hinder the proving process (see Glossary).

3. Preheat the oven to 100°F (40°C)—when it reaches that temperature turn it off. Place the croissant dough inside to rise. Make sure the temperature doesn't exceed 100°F (40°C) because if it is too hot the butter will start to withdraw from the dough and make the croissant dull and without flakiness. The croissant will need to rise ¾ larger than its initial size and this will probably take 40 minutes to 1 hour. When risen, remove from the oven.

4. Preheat the oven to 345°F (175°C/Gas Mark 4). Slightly egg wash (see Glossary) the croissants using a pastry brush. Bake the croissants in the middle of the oven for 20–25 minutes, until golden, crispy and flaky. Turn the tray halfway when baking as this will help the croissant to bake evenly. Remove from the oven and serve warm, ideally within 4 hours.

CROISSANT BREAD AND BUTTER PUDDING

Pudding au Croissant

MAKES 4

A great way to use leftover croissants to create a fantastic dessert with ease.

1. PREPARE THE FILLING

In a saucepan, boil the milk, cream, rum and sultanas over medium heat. In a separate bowl, mix the eggs and sugar. When the milk mixture is at boiling point, add it to the egg mixture, whisking it continuously. Add the vanilla essence and diced croissant. Set it aside to soak for 1 minute.

2. ASSEMBLE, BAKE AND SERVE

Preheat the oven to 345°F (175°C/Gas Mark 4). Line each mould with baking paper for easy unmoulding. Scoop out the soaked croissant pieces and divide evenly between the moulds. Pour the leftover liquid on top of the croissant pieces, making sure the sultanas are scattered evenly throughout. Bake for 15–20 minutes. After baking, the puddings should be just set with a touch of liquid remaining when they are pressed on top. Serve immediately with double cream or ice cream.

4fl oz (125ml) milk

4fl oz (125ml) pouring cream

½fl oz (15ml) rum

1½oz (40g) sultanas (or diced dry fruit)

3 eggs (1¾–2oz/50–55g each)

2oz (60g) superfine/caster sugar

1 teaspoon vanilla essence

3 day-old croissants, cut into quarters
   (12 pieces in total)

EQUIPMENT

Mixing bowl, 8in (20cm) diameter

Saucepan, 8in (20cm) diameter

Baking tray

4 rectangular moulds, 5in (12cm) x 2½in
   (6cm) x 1¾in (4cm)

Whisk

Knife

Baking tray

Baking paper

TIPS AND TRICKS

The sultanas are boiled with the milk and cream so they puff up and become juicer, rather than dull and dry.

Croissant Dough

CHOCOLATE CROISSANT
Pain au Chocolat

MAKES 6

When in Paris, nothing is better than a chocolate croissant with a steaming bowl of coffee for breakfast.

1 quantity (24oz/675g) Croissant Dough
  (see recipe)
2½oz (80g) milk or dark chocolate (4 squares
  of a chocolate block)
1 egg for egg wash

EQUIPMENT
Rolling pin
Baking tray
Baking paper
Knife
Pastry brush

1. PREPARE THE CROISSANT DOUGH

Lightly flour a bench top. Using a rolling pin, roll the dough to 15in (38cm) x 12in (30cm) in size, then cut 6 strips of 2½in (6cm) x 12in (30cm). Place about ⅙oz (5g) chocolate in a line at the end of each strip then fold down 3 times. Add another ⅙oz (5g) chocolate then keep rolling—leave a ½in (1cm) gap at the end of the strip. Brush some egg wash on the gap to seal the bottom fold. Place on a baking tray. Keep the fold under the croissant otherwise it will unravel when proving (see Glossary).

2. PROVE THE DOUGH

Preheat the oven to 100°F (40°C)—when it reaches that temperature turn it off. Place the chocolate croissant inside to rise. Make sure the temperature doesn't exceed 100°F (40°C) because if it is too hot the butter will start to withdraw from the dough and make the chocolate croissant dull and without flakiness. The chocolate croissant will need to rise, larger than its initial size and this will probably take 40 minutes to 1 hour. When risen, remove from the oven.

3. ASSEMBLE, BAKE AND SERVE

Preheat the oven to 345°F (175°C/Gas Mark 4). Slightly egg wash (see Glossary) the chocolate croissants using a pastry brush. Bake in the middle of the oven for 20–25 minutes, until golden, crispy and flaky. Turn the tray halfway when baking as this will help the chocolate croissant to bake evenly.

Remove from the oven and serve warm, ideally within 4 hours.

Croissant Dough

RHUBARB DANISH
Danish à la Rhubarbe

MAKES 8

This fabulous danish celebrates the wonderful flavours of rhubarb—apples or seasonal fruit can be used as substitutes.

1. PREPARE THE RHUBARB COMPOTE

Cut the rhubarb into 1¾in (4cm) batons, put into a mixing bowl and toss with sugar. Transfer ingredients to a saucepan and add the wine. Place over low to medium heat and keep stirring with a wooden spoon until all the sugar has dissolved and the mixture starts to break down—the end result should still have large chunks of softened rhubarb. Place on a plate, cover with plastic wrap to seal freshness and store in the refrigerator. The compote can be stored in the refrigerator for 3 days; it cannot be frozen.

2. PREPARE THE DANISH DOUGH

Lightly flour a benchtop. Using a rolling pin, roll out the dough to 12in (30cm) x 15in (38cm) then cut 8 squares of 2¾in (7cm) x 3¾in (9cm) each. Fold each corner back into the centre to create a classic Danish look. Be sure to press the centre in firmly, otherwise the folds will unravel during the proving process (see Glossary). Place on a baking tray. Preheat the oven to 100°F (40°C/Gas Mark ½)—when it reaches that temperature turn the oven off. Place the dough inside to rise. The danish will need to rise ¾ larger than its initial size and this will probably take 40 minutes to 1 hour. Once proved, remove from oven.

3. ASSEMBLE, BAKE AND SERVE

Preheat the oven to 345°F (175°C/Gas Mark 4). Brush egg wash on the top of each danish and add 1 teaspoon (⅓oz/10g) crème pâtissière, then 1 tablespoon (1oz/30g) rhubarb compote. Bake for 15–20 minutes or until the danish is golden—serve immediately.

RHUBARB COMPOTE

Makes 7½oz (220g)

9oz (250g) fresh rhubarb, 3 to 4 stems

1oz (30g) superfine/caster sugar

2½fl oz (80ml) white wine

1 quantity (24oz/675g) Croissant Dough (see recipe)

1 egg for egg wash

1 quantity (10½oz/300g) Crème Pâtissière (see Vanilla Slice)

EQUIPMENT

Mixing bowl, 8in (20cm)

Saucepan, 8in (20cm) diameter

Wooden spoon

Plate

Rolling pin

Knife

Plastic wrap

Baking tray

Pastry brush

Teaspoon

Tablespoon

Croissant Dough

ALMOND CROISSANT
Croissant aux Amandes

MAKES 6

To make almond croissant, we recommend using a day-old croissant as they are drier and easier to handle.

SYRUP

8fl oz (250ml) water

4oz (125g) superfine/caster sugar

1fl oz (30ml) dark rum

²⁄3oz (20g) Almond Cream (see Galette recipe)

1 quantity (24oz/675g) day-old croissants from Croissant Dough (see recipe)

²⁄3oz (20g) sliced almond, unroasted

EQUIPMENT

Saucepan, 8in (20cm) diameter

Serrated knife

Cooling rack

Pastry brush

Spoon

Baking tray

Baking paper

Tablespoon

1. PREPARE THE SYRUP

In a saucepan, combine the water and sugar over a medium heat and bring to the boil. Remove pan from the heat and stir in the rum. Set aside at room temperature.

2. ASSEMBLE, BAKE AND SERVE

Preheat the oven to 340°F (170°C/Gas Mark 3). Take the croissants (or chocolate croissant) and cut in half with a serrated knife, starting from the front part until almost through to the back, then open out the croissant. Brush generously with the syrup until the pastry is soft to touch. Place 1–2 tablespoons almond cream in the middle of the croissant, spread out, then close the croissant. Place a fine line of almond cream on top of the croissant—about ¹⁄3oz (10g) on each—then place some sliced almonds on top. Set on a baking tray lined with baking paper. Bake croissants for 15 minutes or until the almond cream and almonds are golden. Serve immediately.

CROISSANT BASKET WITH BERRIES

Puit de Fruits Frais

Makes 8

This wonderful recipe uses spare puff pastry and will impress your guests—the fruit used can be matched to the season.

1. PREPARE THE CHANTILLY CREAM

In a mixing bowl, whip the cream to ribbon stage (see Glossary). Start adding the sugar, continue whisking, and then add the vanilla essence. This cream should last up to 3 days in the refrigerator—if it loses structure, whisk it back to normal consistency.

2. ASSEMBLE, BAKE AND SERVE

Lightly flour a bench top. Using a rolling pin, roll the dough to a 15in (38cm) x 16in (40cm) rectangle then cut 8 squares, each 3–3¾in (8–9cm) in size. Lightly egg wash each square, then sprinkle some raw sugar on the top. Turn the muffin moulds upside down and butter and flour the bottom. Place each square (sugar facing up) onto the upside down mould so that the pastry square covers each mound to form an upside down basket. Preheat the oven to 345°F (175°C/Gas Mark 4). Bake for 20 minutes. Remove baskets from the mould and set right side up on a baking tray, then bake for a further 5 minutes. Remove from the oven and allow to cool then place 1 tablespoon chantilly cream in each, filling ¾ of each basket, then add the seasonal fruit.

1 quantity (24oz/675g) Croissant Dough
   (see recipe)
1 egg for egg wash
1¾oz (50g) raw sugar
14oz (400g) seasonal fruit

CRÈME CHANTILLY

8fl oz (250ml) pouring cream
1¾oz (50g) superfine/caster sugar
1 teaspoon vanilla essence

EQUIPMENT

Mixing bowl, 8in (20cm)
Whisk
Rolling pin
Knife
8 muffin moulds, 2¾in (7cm) diameter x
   1¾in (4cm) high
Pastry brush
Baking tray
Baking paper
Tablespoon

TIPS AND TRICKS

You can use any seasonal fruit such as mango, berries or stonefruit.

Croissant Dough

Choux Pastry

Pâte à Choux

CHOUX PASTRY
Pâte à Choux

MAKES 21OZ (600G)

The most versatile of all doughs, choux can be served savoury, sweet, baked or fried.

Makes 21oz (600g)

3½ oz (100g) unsalted butter, soft

4fl oz (125ml) water

4fl oz (125ml) milk

¹/₆oz (5g) superfine/caster sugar

¹/₈oz (3g) table salt

5oz (150g) all-purpose/plain flour

4 eggs (1¾–2oz/50–55g each)

1. Have your electric mixer ready with the bowl and paddle attachment.

2. Place butter, water, milk, sugar and salt into a saucepan over a medium heat and bring to the boil. Add all the flour and, using a wooden spoon, stir the mixture constantly until a skin is formed on the bottom of the saucepan—about 2 minutes.

3. Transfer the mixture to the bowl on the electric mixer and mix at medium speed. Where there is no more steam rising from the dough—about 1 minute—gradually add the eggs one by one. Continue mixing until all the eggs have been incorporated and then mix for a further 1 minute.

4. Transfer the dough onto a plate and cover with plastic wrap. Make sure the plastic wrap is in direct contact with the surface of the dough otherwise it will form a skin. Refrigerate for 20 minutes until it becomes firm, then follow recipe for baking.

EQUIPMENT

Electric mixer with paddle attachment

Saucepan, 8in (20cm) diameter—no teflon

Wooden spoon

Plate

Plastic wrap

TIPS AND TRICKS

Before piping the choux pastry, spray the baking tray lightly with oil and then line with baking paper—this will stop the paper from lifting when you are piping.

Make an egg wash and dip a fork into it—then make a cross pattern on the top of each ball, pressing lightly. If you press too hard, the choux ball will cook.

To pipe balls of choux, hold the piping nozzle ½–⅔in (1–1.5cm) above the tray at a 90-degree angle. Gently squeeze the piping bag and pipe the desired size. Release the pressure and cut the end off the ball with a sideways flicking movement.

Never open the oven door for the first 8 minutes of cooking otherwise the choux will collapse.

A properly baked choux should be golden brown and dried out—if the choux is not properly dried, it will collapse.

All choux products, once baked, are best eaten within 4 hours.

CHOCOLATE ÉCLAIR
Éclair au Chocolat

MAKES 8

Everyone's favourite—the éclair can have numerous fillings; however, chocolate is an all-time classic.

SABLE TOPPING

2½oz (80g) unsalted butter, soft

3½ oz (100g) raw sugar

3½ oz (100g) all-purpose/plain flour

1 teaspoon vanilla essence

CHOCOLATE GLAZE

1/6oz (5g) gelatine leaves (1.5 leaves)

1¾fl oz (50ml) pouring cream

3oz (90g) superfine/caster sugar

2¼fl oz (70ml) water, tap and cold

1oz (30g) Dutch cocoa powder

½ quantity 10½oz (300g) Choux Pastry dough (see recipe)

1 quantity (10½oz/300g) Crème Pâtissière (see Vanilla Slice)

EQUIPMENT

DOUGH

3 piping bags

Piping nozzle, round, no. 808

Piping nozzle, round, no. 804

Ribbon nozzle

Baking tray

1. PREPARE THE CHOUX PASTRY

Place the choux dough into a piping bag with nozzle no. 808 and then pipe into 6in (15cm) long strips onto a baking tray lined with baking paper. To do this, hold the bag at a 45-degree angle to the tray and gently squeeze while dragging the tube along the tray in a straight 6in (15cm) line. When you get to the end of the éclair, stop applying pressure and pivot the piping bag to a 90-degree angle in a downwards motion, then drag the bag away from the éclair. Repeat to make remaining éclairs, spacing them at least 1¾in (4cm) apart—they should weigh about 1½oz (45g) each.

2. PREPARE THE SABLE TOPPING

Place the butter and sugar in a mixing bowl and mix with your fingertips until combined. Add the flour and vanilla, and continue mixing until a dough has formed. Roll 6½oz (185g) dough between 2 sheets of A4 size baking paper—the dough should not be thicker than ⅛in (2mm). Any excess dough can be frozen and kept for up to 1 month. Freeze the dough sheet for 20 minutes. Then, using a serrated knife, slice the sheets into strips 6in (15cm) long x 1¾in (4cm) wide. Freeze again before use.

3. PREPARE THE CHOCOLATE GLAZE

Soften the gelatine in cold water in a bowl, making sure the leaves are completely submerged. In a small pot over a medium heat, boil the cream, sugar and water, then remove pot from the heat. Squeeze the gelatine to remove the water and whisk into the cream mixture. Add the cocoa powder and continue whisking. Pass the mixture through a sieve (see Glossary) into a bowl. Cover the surface with plastic wrap otherwise it will develop a skin which can cause unsightly lumps in the mixture. Place in the refrigerator to set.

4. ASSEMBLE, BAKE AND SERVE

Preheat the oven to 345°F (175°C/Gas Mark 4). Take the baking tray with the piped éclairs and place a strip of sable on top of each éclair. Bake for 20–25 minutes. Remove from the oven and cool. Using a wooden stick, make 3 evenly spaced holes along the top of the éclair. Whisk the crème pâtissière in a bowl to regain a smooth consistency. Using a piping bag with no. 804 nozzle, pipe the crème pâtissière into each of the éclairs until full.

To decorate, whisk the chocolate glaze until a smooth pipeable texture is achieved. Fill a piping bag with a ribbon attachment and pipe a strip of glaze along the top of the éclair.

Baking paper
2 mixing bowls, 8in (20cm) diameter
2 whisks
Spoon
Wooden stick (pencil thickness)
Plastic wrap

SABLE
Mixing bowl, 8in (20cm)
Rolling pin
Serrated knife
2 sheets A4 size baking paper

CHOCOLATE GLAZE
2 mixing bowls, 8in (20cm) diameter
Saucepan, 8in (20cm)
Whisk
Sieve
Plastic wrap
Piping bag
Piping nozzle, ribbon, 1in (2.5cm)

Choux Pastry

TEMPERING CHOCOLATE THE EASY WAY

Chocolate transfers can only be purchased from commercial suppliers; however, you can make any shapes for decoration yourself, using tempered chocolate. Chocolate transfer sheets are made from cocoa butter mixed with food colourings to make patterns and are used in pâtisseries all over the world. Following is a simple recipe for tempering chocolate to create a chocolate transfer.

Place 10½oz (300g) of the chocolate in a bowl over a bain marie (see Glossary) at 90–100°F (30–35°C).

While stirring, melt the chocolate until no chocolate pieces are visible then remove from the heat.

Add the remaining 3oz (90g) chocolate and mix with the flexible spatula until the temperature drops to 85–88°F (30–31°C). Note: if using milk or white chocolate, reduce the temperature to 82–84°F (28–29°C).

Pour the now tempered chocolate onto the plain, clear plastic sleeves or chocolate transfer placed on a flat tray that fits into the refrigerator. Spread the chocolate with the palette knife to an even thickness, about ⅛in (3mm). Allow the chocolate to partially set, then score (see Glossary) with a knife and cut 6in (15cm) x 1in (2.5cm) rectangles—the same size as the sable, to accommodate the shape of the éclair. Cover with another sheet of clear plastic sleeve, place a flat weight (e.g. a baking tray) on top to reduce the chocolate curling. Leave in the refrigerator to set for 10 minutes or more. Remove strips one by one from the sheet and place on top of each éclair.

13½ oz (390g) dark couverture chocolate (70% cocoa), chopped

EQUIPMENT

Saucepan, 6in (15cm) diameter

Mixing bowl, 8in (20cm) diameter

Flexible spatula

Clear plastic sleeves or 2 chocolate transfer sheets

Palette knife

Ruler

Digital thermometer

Chopping board

Knife

Baking paper

Baking tray

TIPS AND TRICKS

Always use couverture chocolate for tempering.

To check tempering: dip a piece of baking paper into the melted chocolate—you should be able to see the chocolate set after leaving it for 2 minutes.

 Choux Pastry

CHOUX PASTRY DISC
Corniotte

MAKES 15

A speciality from Burgundy where Vincent was born—it is found in every village fair.

1 quantity (14oz/400g) Sweet Dough
  (see recipe)

1 quantity (21oz/600g) Choux Pastry dough
  (see recipe)

3½ oz (100g) pearl sugar or raw sugar

EQUIPMENT

Rolling pin

Baking paper

Baking tray

Cutter, round, 3¼in (8cm)

Piping bag and nozzle no. 804

Fork

1. PREPARE THE SWEET PASTRY
Lightly flour a bench top. Roll the sweet dough, using a rolling pin, until ¼in (5mm) thick. Dock the dough (see Glossary). Using a cutter, cut 15 discs and place them on a baking tray lined with baking paper.

2. PREPARE THE CHOUX DOUGH
Put the choux dough into a piping bag with nozzle no. 804 and pipe a spiral of choux to cover the sweet pastry disc. Sprinkle sugar on top of the choux—they can be frozen, unbaked, for 1 month.

3. BAKE AND SERVE
Preheat the oven to 340°F (170°C/Gas Mark 3). Bake for 15–20 minutes or until golden brown and serve immediately.

PARIS-BREST

Paris-Brest

MAKES 8 INDIVIDUAL

Paris-Brest was created in 1891 to commemorate the first bicycle race from Paris to Brest and back to Paris—it is of a circular shape to represent a bicycle wheel.

1. PREPARE THE CHOUX PASTRY

Cut 1 sheet of baking paper into an 8in (20cm) x 12in (30cm) rectangle. Using a marker pen and the cutter for tracing, draw eight 3¼in (8cm) rings, ¾in (2cm) apart, on the sheet. Spray the baking tray with oil and place the sheet of baking paper, ink side down, on it. Place the choux dough in a piping bag with nozzle no. 808 and pipe a ring of dough on each stencil. Sprinkle about ⅙oz (5g) of sliced almonds on each ring of choux.

2. PREPARE THE MOUSSELINE CREAM

Place the crème pâtissière into a bowl and whisk to a smooth consistency. Add the softened butter and hazelnut paste, and whisk to combine. Set aside in the refrigerator.

3. ASSEMBLE, BAKE AND SERVE

Preheat the oven to 345°F (175°C/Gas Mark 4). Bake the choux rings for about 20 minutes. Remove from the oven and cool. Cut each ring in half horizontally. Place the mousseline cream into the piping bag with the star nozzle and pipe a ring of cream on top of the bottom half of the choux ring—about 4⅓oz (130g) each. Sprinkle the crushed nougatine on top of the cream. Place the top of the choux ring on the mousseline cream and dust with icing sugar. Serve immediately.

TIPS AND TRICKS

Any type of nuts can be substituted for the sliced almonds.
If hazelnut paste is not available, substitute with Nutella.

½ quantity (10½oz/300g) Choux Pastry
  dough (see recipe)
1½oz (40g) almonds, sliced (or mixed nuts)
1¾oz (50g) nougatine, crushed (see recipe)
3½oz (100g) confectioner's/icing sugar for
  dusting
oil for spraying

MOUSSELINE CREAM

1 quantity (10½oz/300g) Crème Pâtissière
  (see Vanilla Slice)
21oz (600g) unsalted butter, softened
4oz (120g) spreadable hazelnut paste

EQUIPMENT

Scissors
Baking paper
Baking tray
Marker pen
2 piping bags
Piping nozzle, round, no. 808
Piping nozzle, star, no. 828
Mixing bowl, 8in (20cm) diameter
Cutter, round, 3¼in (8cm)
Serrated knife
Whisk

Choux Pastry

CHEESE PUFFS

Gougères

MAKES 80

Gougères are fabulous puffs of pastry filled with cheese. They are said to have originated from Sens in Burgundy, a region producing brilliant white wines.

BÈCHAMEL FILLING

Makes 16oz (450g)

1oz (30g) unsalted butter

2¼oz (70g) all-purpose/plain flour

10¼fl oz (300ml) milk

2½ oz (75g) goat's cheese

¼oz (8g) blue cheese

2 egg yolks

4 pinches salt

3 pinches pepper

1 quantity (21oz/600g) Choux Pastry dough (see recipe)

1½oz (45g) Parmesan, shredded or grated

1 egg for eggwash

EQUIPMENT

2 saucepans, 8in (20cm) diameter

Whisk

2 piping bags

Piping nozzle no. 804

Piping nozzle no. 803

Wooden stick (pencil thickness)

Fork

Baking tray

Baking paper

1. PREPARE THE BÈCHAMEL FILLING

Melt the butter in a saucepan on a stovetop over medium heat and boil until it reaches a golden brown colour. Add all the flour and whisk for 1 minute, this will cook out the flour—the mixture should look like a crumble. Add half the milk while whisking. Once the mixture is smooth, remove from the heat and whisk in the rest of the milk, goat's cheese, blue cheese, egg yolks and seasonings, then remove from the heat and stir until all combined. Bèchamel can be stored in a container, with plastic wrap directly in contact with the surface to prevent a skin forming, in the refrigerator for up to 3 days—it cannot be frozen.

2. PREPARE THE CHOUX PASTRY

Line a baking tray with baking paper. Put the choux pastry in a piping bag with no. 804 nozzle. Hold the nozzle ½in (1cm) above the tray at a 90-degree angle, gently squeeze the piping bag and pipe a 1in (2.5cm) diameter ball—about ¼oz (7g) each. Repeat until all the choux pastry is used. Dip a fork in the egg wash and gently press into the top of all the choux making a crisscross pattern on the top.

3. ASSEMBLE, BAKE AND SERVE

Preheat the oven to 345°F (175°C/Gas Mark 4). Bake the puffs for 20–25 minutes. Remove from the oven and cool. Pierce the base of each puff with a wooden stick and twist to make a cavity. Place bèchamel sauce in a piping bag with nozzle no. 803 and fill each puff—about ⅙oz (6g) each. Pipe a little more bèchamel on the top of each puff and sprinkle with the Parmesan. They can be set aside at room temperature for up to 1 hour. Reheat the puffs at 345°F (175°C/Gas Mark 4) for 5 minutes—serve immediately while still warm.

CROQUEMBOUCHE

Croquembouche

MAKES 1 TOWER (50 BALLS)

The croquembouche—meaning 'crunch in the mouth'—was created by Marie-Antoine Câreme and is traditionally served at weddings and christenings. Other decorations can be marzipan sweets, sugar coated fruit and dragee, which are sugared almonds, or angel hair (spun sugar).

CARAMEL TOPPING CRÈME

3½ oz (100g) glucose

14oz (400g) superfine/caster sugar

2fl oz (60ml) water

1½ quantities (32oz/900g) Choux Pastry
*   dough (see recipe)*

1 egg for egg wash

1 quantity (10½oz/300g) Crème Pâtissière
*   (see Vanilla Slice)*

3½ oz (100g) sugared almonds

EQUIPMENT

2 piping bags

Piping nozzle, round, no. 806

Piping nozzle, round, no. 803

Fork

Wooden stick (pencil thickness)

Mixing bowl, 8in (20cm)

Saucepan, 8in (20cm)

Whisk

Baking tray

Baking paper

Foam cone—4½in (11.5cm) diameter base x
*   10in (25cm) high*

1. PREPARE THE CHOUX PASTRY

Preheat the oven to 340°F (170°C/Gas Mark 3). Line a baking tray with baking paper. Place the choux dough into the piping bag with nozzle no. 806 and pipe 1½in (3.5cm) diameter balls—about ²⁄₃oz (20g) each—onto the baking tray, making sure you set them well apart as they will expand during cooking. Dip a fork in the egg wash and gently press into the top of each choux, making a crisscross pattern. Bake for 20 minutes. Remove from the oven and set aside to cool.

Puncture the base of each choux ball with a wooden stick and make a cavity. Place the crème pâtissière in a bowl and whisk to a smooth consistency. Place the crème pâtissière in a piping bag with nozzle no. 803 and fill each of the choux balls—about ¹⁄₃oz (10g) each.

2. PREPARE THE CARAMEL TOPPING

Place the glucose, sugar and water in a saucepan, and mix until all the sugar is wet. With a wet pastry brush, wash down the sides of the saucepan to remove any excess sugar around the edges, otherwise the sugar may crystallise. Bring to the boil and cook until light honey in colour (about 310–325°F/155–160°C) without stirring. Remove the caramel from the heat, and leave for 5 minutes as the caramel will thicken a little and make it easier for coating as well as continue to darken in colour.

Line a baking tray with baking paper. Take a choux ball and dip the top into the caramel topping (maximum ½in/1cm)—don't dip your fingers in or they will burn! Lift the choux away from the caramel and gently scrape the dripping strand of caramel on the side of the pot. Place the choux ball, caramel side up, on the baking tray. Continue until all the choux are glazed, then set aside. Remember that the caramel will continue to colour off the stove.

3. PREPARE THE TOWER

Wrap baking paper around the whole surface of the foam cone and tape down with masking tape.

Place a smear of caramel in the centre of the base of the cone and stick it to the centre of the cake board to prevent the cone from moving. By now the caramel should have set on the choux balls. Take the first two choux balls, dip the side of one into the caramel and place at the base of the cone directly against the board with the fresh caramel facing to the side so that is is not in contact with the board. Before the caramel sets, place the second choux ball next to the first, making sure that the fresh caramel is in contact with the second choux. Hold in place for a few minutes to ensure that the caramel is completely set—if this is not done, the choux will warp and not stick, possibly collapsing when unmoulding. Take a third choux ball, dip a side into the caramel and stick next to the second choux along the base. Continue this process until the base of the cone has a ring of choux. The base ring of choux must be set fully before starting on the next ring. Remember you are joining the choux balls together, not joining the choux with caramel to the board.

When there are about 4 choux left to complete the base ring, take 4 unattached choux and make sure that these fit nicely to complete the ring without any gaps or overlap. If they don't, sort through the choux to find the right sized ball to make a neat ring. You will need to repeat this checking process near the end of each ring.

Cake board, 8in (20cm) diameter

Display stand, 10in (25cm) diameter

Knife

Pastry brush

Masking tape

Choux Pastry

4. COMPLETING THE TOWER

Create the second layer of the ring by following the same steps as the first ring, remembering that every choux from now onwards needs to be dipped in caramel on the bottom half as well as the side and joined to every adjacent choux with caramel—making sure the fresh caramel is in contact with the two choux in the ring below and the first choux of this ring.

Continue layering until the tower is complete—leave to fully set. The top of the tower will be a single choux.

5. TO UNMOULD AND DECORATE THE TOWER

Slide the chef's knife between the base ring of choux and the cake board. Gently twist the knife up until the cake board detaches from the cone and the tower. Gently hold the tower in one hand, stick the pointed end of a slim knife in the base of the cone and gently twist—the cone should lift away from the baking paper. Carefully peel the baking paper from the inside of the tower. Using a little more caramel, stick the tower onto the display board or plate—let the caramel set before decorating. To decorate, dip sugared almonds in caramel and fill any larger gaps between the choux balls. Stems of fresh flowers can be simply poked through the gaps in the tower.

TIPS AND TRICKS

If the caramel becomes too cool to work with, reheat it over a low to medium heat—a lower heat is better or you risk darkening the caramel too much and having to start again.

To easily clean a pot with caramel, fill the pot with water to cover all the leftover caramel. Place over a high heat and boil to dissolve the hard caramel.

Be very careful when using the hot caramel topping—it can cause injury if it comes into contact with your body.

When using hot caramel topping, work near the sink. If you burn your skin, run the area of skin under cold water for at least 10 minutes. Seek medical advice immediately afterward if necessary.

The croquembouche can be stored for a maximum 12 hours in a refrigerator—the longer it stays refrigerated, the stickier the caramel will be and eventually it will start to dissolve.

Choux Pastry

HOW TO MAKE ANGEL HAIR

Set the box over the sink. Have the whisk or forks and the wooden spoon next to the box. Heat the caramel topping until it reaches pouring consistency—when a fork is dipped into it and lifted up, the caramel should pour steadily from the fork without the stream breaking. Take the caramel pot over to the box and, using the whisk (or 2 forks), dip the tip into the caramel, lift up and shake back and forth on top of the box lengthwise. Redip and repeat the process to make thick layers. Gently lift the angel hair from the box and set as a spiral on the tower. The angel hair decoration needs serving within 20 minutes or it will disintegrate. It can be frozen for 24 hours in an airtight container before using.

large box (cardboard or plastic)
leftover caramel (from the croquembouche recipe)

EQUIPMENT
Large cardboard or plastic box, about 12in (30cm) x 6in (15cm) in size, with one long side cut out
Whisk with the end cut off, or 2 forks
Long wooden spoon or flexible spatula

TIPS AND TRICKS
Angel hair should not be used when the weather is very humid, as the high humidity will cause the sugar to dissolve and make the tower unattractive.

 Choux Pastry

NUN'S PASTRY

Religieuse

MAKES 12

This dessert is two choux balls filled with crème pâtissière and set on top of each other. The word religieuse means 'nun'—the top choux represents the nun's head and the bottom choux the nun's body.

Makes 8½oz (240g)

*½ quantity (10½oz/300g) Choux Pastry
   dough (see recipe)*

1 egg for egg wash

*16oz (460g) Crème Pâtissière
   (see Vanilla Slice)*

3½ oz (100g) honey

CARAMELISED CHOCOLATE

7oz (200g) white chocolate, melted

1. PREPARE THE CHOUX PASTRY

Line a baking tray with baking paper. You will need 2 different sized choux balls for each serve. Place the choux dough in the piping bag with the no. 806 nozzle and pipe twelve 1¾in (4cm) diameter balls on the baking tray—about ⅔oz (20g) each. If you have 2 baking trays that can fit into your oven, line another tray with baking paper and pipe twelve 1¼in (3cm) diameter balls on the second tray (use the cutters as a size guide). If you do not have the second tray, make the smaller choux balls after the larger balls are baked. Dip a fork in the egg wash and gently press on the top of the choux. Preheat the oven to 345°F (175°C/Gas Mark 4). Bake the larger balls for 20–25 minutes and the smaller balls for 15–20 minutes. Remove from the oven and cool. Using the wooden stick, make a hole in the base of each ball by twisting a wooden stick.

2. PREPARE THE CARAMELISED CHOCOLATE

Preheat the oven to 340°F (170°C/Gas Mark 3). Line a baking tray with baking paper and, using a spatula, spread the melted white chocolate in an even layer. Place in the oven and as the chocolate cooks it will start to caramelise around the edges. At this point— the chocolate will start to take on a grainy/sandy like texture— stir the mixture together on the tray and continue baking. Repeat this process until all the chocolate is granulated and a light caramel colour. Remove from oven and cool. Dice chocolate if chunks are too large. It can be stored in an airtight container for 1 week.

EQUIPMENT

Baking tray

Baking paper

Piping bag

Piping nozzle no. 806

Fork

Wooden stick (pencil thickness)

Pastry brush

Piping nozzle no. 801

Rolling pin

Cutter, 1¾in (4cm) diameter

Cutter, 1¼in (3cm) diameter

Spatula

Saucepan, 6in (15cm) diameter

TIPS AND TRICKS

Only use couverture for the white chocolate.

3. ASSEMBLE AND SERVE

Place the crème pâtissière into the piping bag with nozzle no. 801 and fill each of the large and small balls—you should have extra left in the bag for decoration. Place the caramelised chocolate in a bowl or tray. Heat the honey slightly on the stove top and brush the top of each ball lightly with honey. Dip each of the balls in the caramelised chocolate—about ⅓oz (10g) each. Pipe a small knob of crème pâtissière on the top of each larger choux and sit the smaller choux on top. Pipe vertical strips of crème pâtissière, starting from the top of the larger choux to hide the join to the smaller choux.

ST HONORÉ

St Honoré

MAKES 12

The St Honoré was named after the Catholic patron saint of bakers and pastry chefs.

1. PREPARE THE PUFF PASTRY

Preheat the oven to 345°F (175°C/Gas Mark 4). Lightly flour a bench top. Line a baking tray with baking paper. Using a rolling pin, roll the dough to a 16in (40cm) x 12in (30cm) rectangle. Place the puff pastry sheet on the baking tray and place small moulds on each of the corners to make the height ¾in (2cm). Place the cake rack on top to stop the pastry from rising too much. Bake for 25 minutes then reduce the temperature to 340°F (170°C/Gas Mark 3) and bake for a further 10 minutes. Remove from the oven and allow the puff sheet to cool. Using the serrated knife, cut the sheet into twelve 2½in (6cm) x 5in (12cm) rectangles. Set aside.

2. PREPARE THE CHOUX PASTRY

Place the choux dough into the piping bag with nozzle no. 804 and pipe thirty-six 1in (2.5cm) choux balls onto a baking tray lined with baking paper. Dip a fork into the egg wash and gently press into the top of each of the balls. Bake at 345°F (175°C/Gas Mark 4) for 15–20 minutes. Remove from oven and cool. Take the wooden stick and puncture the base of each choux ball to make a cavity. Place the crème pâtissière in the piping bag with nozzle no. 803 and fill each of the choux. Glaze the top of each choux with the hot caramel.

3. ASSEMBLE AND SERVE

Place the chantilly cream into the piping bag with no. 804 nozzle. Take 3 choux balls, pipe a small knob of chantilly cream on the bottom of each choux and place on the right side of the puff pastry rectangle, lengthwise in a row. On the left side, pipe a spiral of chantilly cream alongside the row of choux—about ¾oz (25g) each. Repeat for remaining St Honoré. Decorate with caramel if desired. Serve immediately.

1 quantity (24oz/675g) Puff Pastry dough (see recipe)

½ quantity (10½oz/300g) Choux Pastry dough (see recipe)

egg wash 1 egg for egg wash

1 quantity (10½oz/300g) Crème Pâtissière (see Vanilla Slice)

1 quantity (19¾oz/560g) caramel, hot (see Croquembouche recipe)

1 quantity Crème Chantilly (see Croissant Basket with Berries)

EQUIPMENT

Rolling pin

Baking paper

Baking tray

4 tarlet moulds, 2½in (6cm) x ¾in (2cm) high

Cake rack

Serrated knife

2 piping bags

Piping nozzle no. 804

Piping nozzle no. 803

Fork

Wooden stick (pencil thickness)

TIPS AND TRICKS

Drizzle the excess caramel onto baking paper, cut to size and use as decoration.

Choux Pastry

CREAM PUFF
Choux à la Crème

MAKES 12

We all remember growing up with cream buns from the cake shop; this is the French version.

½ quantity (10½oz/300g) Choux Pastry
   dough (see recipe)

1 egg for egg wash

1¾oz (50g) pearl sugar

1 quantity (10½oz/300g) Crème Chantilly
   (see Croissant Basket with Berries)

3½ oz (100g) confectioner's/icing sugar for
   dusting

EQUIPMENT

Piping bag

Piping nozzle no. 806

Piping nozzle, star, no. 828

Baking tray

Baking paper

Fork

Serrated knife

1. PREPARE THE CHOUX PASTRY

Preheat the oven to 345°F (175°C/Gas Mark 4). Line a baking tray with baking paper. Place the choux dough in the piping bag with nozzle no. 806 and pipe twelve 1¾in (4cm) diameter balls onto the baking tray—about ⅔oz (20g) each. Dip your fork in the egg wash and gently press into the top of each of the choux, then sprinkle with pearl sugar. Bake for 15–20 minutes. Remove from oven and allow to cool.

2. ASSEMBLE AND SERVE

Once cooled, cut each of the choux horizontally with the serrated knife. Place the chantilly cream in the piping bag with the star nozzle and pipe a spiral of cream 1½in (3.5cm) high on the base. To do this, hold the piping tube vertically ½in (1cm) above the surface of the choux base and gently squeeze. Move the piping bag in a spiral motion around the choux until you reach the desired height. Put the top half of the choux on top of the cream and dust with confectioner's sugar. Serve immediately.

CHURROS VINCENT-STYLE
Churros

MAKES 15

Churros are a speciality from Spain, traditionally eaten for breakfast and dipped in hot chocolate—this recipe has been given a Vincent twist.

1. PREPARE THE CHURROS

Place the choux dough in the piping bag with the star nozzle. Pour the oil in the larger saucepan—there should be at least 2½in (6cm) of oil. Heat over a high heat to a temperature of 325–340°F (160–175°C). Have the slotted spoon and paper towel on a plate next to the pan.

Carefully pipe four or five 6–8in (15–20cm) strips of dough directly into the hot oil. Hold the bag 2in (5cm) above the surface of the oil and gently squeeze—stop squeezing the bag and use a knife to cut the dough off the nozzle. Do not hold the piping bag too high from the surface of the oil because the hot oil will splash. Do not overcrowd the oil with too many churros otherwise they will stick together. Cook the churros until golden—about 3–4 minutes, turning the churros over once during cooking. Remove the churros from the oil with the slotted spoon and place on the paper towels to drain. Repeat to make remaining churros.

2. PREPARE THE CHOCOLATE DIPPING SAUCE

Place the cream in the smaller saucepan over a medium heat and bring to the boil. Turn off the heat and add both chocolates. Stir with the spatula until all the chocolate is combined, then stir in the butter and set aside.

3. ASSEMBLE AND SERVE

Dust churros with sugar and pile onto a serving plate. Place the ganache into a serving glass and serve with the churros. Serve immediately.

1 quantity (21oz/600g) Choux Pastry dough (see recipe)

32fl oz (1L) vegetable oil for frying

CHOCOLATE DIPPING SAUCE

7fl oz (200ml) pouring cream

1¾oz (50g) milk chocolate, chopped

3½ oz (100g) dark chocolate, chopped

¾oz (25g) butter, softened

1¾oz (50g) confectioner's/icing sugar for dusting

EQUIPMENT

Flexible spatula

Piping bag

Piping nozzle, star, no. 828

Saucepan, 8in (20cm)

Saucepan, 10in (25cm)

Slotted spoon

Paper towel

Flexible spatula

Knife

Choux Pastry

SALTED CARAMEL CHOUX
Choux au Caramel Beurre Salé

MAKES 12

This recipe is easy to make and a hit with young and old thanks to the addition of salted caramel.

1. PREPARE THE CHOUX PASTRY

Preheat the oven to 345°F (175°C/Gas Mark 4). Line a baking tray with baking paper. Place the choux dough in the piping bag with nozzle no. 806 and pipe twelve 1¾in (4cm) diameter balls on the baking tray—about ⅔oz (20g) each. Dip a fork into the eggwash and gently press on the top of each of the balls. Bake for 15–20 minutes. Remove from the oven and cool. Use the wooden stick and puncture the base of each choux to make a cavity.

2. ASSEMBLE AND SERVE

Gently reheat the salted caramel on a stovetop or in a microwave—do not make it hot, just slightly warm to soften into a pouring consistency. Place the crème pâtissière in the mixing bowl and whisk to a smooth consistency, then add the salted caramel and whisk to combine. Place the salted caramel mixture in the piping bag with nozzle no. 803 and fill each of the choux. Glaze each of the choux with the leftover salted caramel and serve immediately.

½ quantity (10½oz/300g) Choux Pastry dough (see recipe)

1 egg for egg wash

7oz (200g) Salted Caramel (see Chocolate & Salted Caramel Tart)

1 quantity (10½oz/300g) Crème Pâtissière (see Vanilla Slice)

EQUIPMENT

Piping bag

Piping nozzle no. 806

Piping nozzle no. 803

Baking tray

Baking paper

Fork

Wooden stick (pencil thickness)

Mixing bowl, 8in (20cm)

Whisk

MINI CHOUX BALLS

Chouquettes

MAKES 40

A must-do when visiting Paris is to visit the neighbourhood pâtisserie and taste their chouquettes—we devour them in about 5 minutes.

½ quantity (10½oz/300g) Choux Pastry
    dough (see recipe)

1 egg for egg wash

3½ oz (100g) pearl sugar or raw sugar

EQUIPMENT

Piping bag

Piping nozzle no. 804

Fork

Baking tray

Baking paper

TIPS AND TRICKS

These chouquettes can also be used as decoration for a croquembouche.

1. PREPARE THE CHOUX PASTRY

Line a baking tray with baking paper. Place the choux dough in the piping bag with nozzle no. 804 and pipe about 40 balls, 1in (2.5cm) in diameter—about ¼oz (7g) each—well apart. Dip a fork into the eggwash and gently press into the top of each of the choux, then lightly press pearl sugar on top.

2. BAKE AND SERVE

Preheat the oven to 345°F (175°C/Gas Mark 4). Bake for 12–15 minutes. Remove from the oven and serve immediately—they will not last long as they are so delicious.

PROFITEROLES

Profiteroles

Serves 9—makes 36 (4 choux per serve)

This easy-to-prepare dessert is filled with ice cream and served with warm chocolate ganache. Profiteroles are quick to prepare for a classic French dinner party.

1. PREPARE THE CHOUX PASTRY

Preheat the oven to 345°F (175°C/Gas Mark 4). Line a baking tray with baking paper. Place the choux dough in the piping bag with nozzle no. 806 and pipe 36 1½in (3.5cm) diameter balls—about ⅔oz (20g) each. Dip a fork into the eggwash and gently press into the top of each of the choux. Bake for 15–20 minutes. Remove from the oven and cool.

2. ASSEMBLE AND SERVE

Cut each choux horizontally with the serrated knife. Fill with a scoop of ice cream and then place the top back on. Place the choux on a serving platter and serve immediately with the warm chocolate glaze.

1 quantity (21oz/600g) Choux Pastry dough

1 egg for egg wash

Ice cream of your choice

Chocolate Glaze (see Chocolate Éclair)

EQUIPMENT

Piping bag

Piping nozzle no. 806

Fork

Baking tray

Baking paper

Serrated knife

Ice cream scoop

Bread Dough

Pâte à Pain

BREAD DOUGH
Pâte à Pain

Bread is essential to our everyday life—in this chapter we have recipes which will surprise you with their simplicity.

17½oz (500g) bakers flour, type 55

2/3oz (20g) yeast, fresh

10¼fl oz (310ml) water, cold

1/3fl oz (10ml) olive oil

1/3oz (10g) table salt

1/6oz (5g) superfine/caster sugar

EQUIPMENT

Electric mixer and hook attachment

Mixing bowl, 8in (20cm)

Plastic wrap

TIPS AND TRICKS

Fresh yeast is preferred for any bread dough making.

During summer, the dough will rise quicker than in winter—in winter place the dough in a warm area to accelerate the proving process.

Give yourself considerable time when making these recipes as there is lag between resting and proving.

1. Place the flour, fresh yeast, water and olive oil into the bowl of an electric mixer.

2. Using the hook attachment, mix the dough on a slow speed then build up to medium speed. Let the dough turn for 6 minutes, then add salt and sugar, then let it turn for a further 4 minutes.

3. Stop the machine, remove the dough and place into a bowl. Wrap with plastic wrap and set aside at room temperature to rise for 20 minutes.

MINI WHITE BAGUETTE

Petite Baguette

MAKES 16 PORTIONS (1¾OZ/50G) EACH

Thinking of France conjures up memories of people queuing at boulangerie for their crusty baguettes—this is an easy at-home version.

1 quantity (30oz/860g) Bread Dough
(see recipe)

flour for dusting

¹/₃oz (10g) table salt

7fl oz (200ml) water, cold

EQUIPMENT

Serrated knife

Rolling pin

2 mixing bowls, 4in (10cm) diameter

2 baking trays

Baking paper

Pastry brush

Plastic wrap

TIPS AND TRICKS

To ensure freshness, make these baguettes
as close to serving time as you can.

1. PREPARE THE BREAD DOUGH

After the dough has rested for 20 minutes and risen, roll the dough with your hands into a log, on a lightly floured bench top, to a length of 20in (50cm), cut it in half lengthwise then cut into 8 portions (16 portions in total).

Roll each portion to 6in (15cm) in length. Once all 12 are completed, repeat the process, lengthening to 10in (25cm) for each baguette—rolling in stages will help the bread to relax, which reduces the dough from shrinking. Line 2 baking trays with baking paper, and place six baguettes on each tray. Preheat the oven to 110°F (50°C/Gas Mark ¼) and when it reaches that temperature turn it off. Place both trays inside to allow the bread to rise, about 30–40 minutes. Remove the trays from the oven and set aside.

Preheat the oven to 350°F (180°C/Gas Mark 4). Place a small metal mixing bowl filled halfway with water at the bottom of the oven as this will create moisture inside the oven (which prevents the bread from drying out quickly). In a bowl dissolve the salt in the water. Lightly brush each baguette with the salted water then dust the top of each with flour. Using a sharp serrated knife, gently slice 3 strips, ¹/₈–¼in (2–5mm) deep, onto each baguette at a 45 degree angle.

2. BAKE AND SERVE

Bake the baguettes at 350°F (180°C/Gas Mark 4) for 18 minutes until golden and crispy. Remove from the oven and leave at room temperature. It is best to serve within 4 hours to ensure freshness. If you wish to serve the baguettes warm, reheat them in the oven at 340°F (170°C/Gas Mark 3) for 5–8 minutes.

WHITE BREAD LOAF
Pain de Mie

MAKES 2 LOAVES

This is a classic white loaf—easy to make at home.

softened butter for greasing

3½ oz (100g) flour for dusting

1 quantity (30oz/860g) Bread Dough

   (see recipe)

⅓oz (10g) table salt

7fl oz (200ml) water, cold

EQUIPMENT

Rolling pin

2 bread loaf tins, 10in (25cm) x 3¾in (9cm)

   x 3¼in (8cm) deep

Baking paper

2 mixing bowls, 4in (10cm) diameter

Pastry brush

TIPS AND TRICKS

To make a seeded bread loaf, use this
recipe and add 2½oz (75g) sunflower
seeds and 2½oz (75g) pumpkin seeds.
Knead in seeds before dividing dough and
you can also sprinkle seeds for decoration
on top before baking.

1. PREPARE THE BREAD DOUGH

Grease 2 bread tins with butter and line with baking paper. After
the dough has rested for 20 minutes and risen, divide the dough
into 2 portions—about 14½oz (430g) each. On a lightly floured
bench top, using a rolling pin, roll each portion to 9in (22cm)
long then place into a loaf tin. Preheat the oven to 110°F (50°C/
Gas Mark ¼) and when it reaches that temperature turn it off.
Place both tins in the oven to allow the bread to rise—about
40–60 minutes—the loaves should double in size. Remove from
the oven and set aside.

2. BAKE AND SERVE

Preheat the oven to 350°F (180°C/Gas Mark 4) full fan. Place a
small metal mixing bowl filled halfway with water at the bottom
of the oven as this will create moisture inside the oven (which
prevents the bread from drying out quickly). In a bowl dissolve
the salt in the water. Lightly brush the top of the loaves with
salted water and then dust with flour. Bake for 20–25 minutes
until golden. When you tap the top of the bread, it should
sound hollow—this means it is ready. Serve warm or at room
temperature. It can be kept frozen for 1 month.

LAVOCHE

Lavoche

Makes 10oz (290g)

Lavoche is fabulous to serve with cheese and easily stored in an airtight container for easy use.

1. Prepare the bread dough

Place the flour and salt in the bowl of an electic mixer. Using the hook attachment, start mixing on a low speed then add melted butter, egg and milk and increase to a medium speed. Let the mixture turn at medium speed for 8 minutes then add the poppy and sesame seeds and turn for a further 2 minutes. Remove the dough and place between 2 sheets of plastic wrap, then flatten it out so it will cool quicker—let it rest in the refrigerator for 1 hour.

2. Assemble, bake and serve

Preheat the oven to 340°F (170°C/Gas Mark 3). After the dough has been rested, place on a lightly floured bench top and using a rolling pin, roll into a 12in (30cm) x 16in (40cm) rectangle. The dough should be fine enough so you can see your fingers underneath it—the finer, the better. Line a baking tray with baking paper and place the dough on the top. Bake for 20–25 minutes until light golden. Remove from the oven and allow to cool. Break the lavoche into chunks about 2in (5cm) x 4in (10cm) then serve with cheese and quince paste or poached pear (see Pear Bourdaloue recipe).

6oz (170g) all-purpose/plain flour

¼oz (7g) table salt

1¼oz (35g) unsalted butter, melted

1 egg (1¾–2oz/50–55g)

1¼fl oz (35ml) milk

¹/3oz (10g) poppy seeds

¹/3oz (10g) sesame seeds

EQUIPMENT

Electric mixer and hook attachment

Plastic wrap

Rolling pin

Baking tray

Baking paper

Bread Dough

BROWN BREAD LOAVES
Pain Brun

MAKES 2 LOAVES

This is a very versatile recipe and can also be adapted to make fruit bread and served with cheese.

I. PREPARE THE BREAD DOUGH

Place the flours, fresh yeast, water and olive oil into the bowl of an electric mixer. Using the hook attachment, mix on a slow speed then build up to medium speed. Let the dough turn at medium speed for 6 minutes. Add salt, then let it turn for a further 4 minutes. Stop the machine, remove the dough and place into the mixing bowl. Wrap with plastic wrap and set it aside at room temperature to rise for 20 minutes.

2. BAKE AND SERVE

Grease 2 bread tins with butter and line with baking paper. Take the risen bread dough and divide it into 2 portions—about 14½oz (430g) each. Roll each loaf to 9in (22cm) long then place into a bread tin. Mix table salt and water in a small bowl and brush on the top of the bread loaves. Dust with flour.

Preheat the oven to 110°F (50°C/Gas Mark ¼) and when it reaches that temperature turn it off. Place both tins in the oven to allow the bread to rise—about 40–60 minutes. The loaves should double in size. Remove from the oven and set aside.

Preheat the oven to 340°F (170°C/Gas Mark 3). Bake loaves for 20–25 minutes. Remove the loaves from the oven and leave at room temperature. It is best to serve within 4 hours to ensure freshness. If you wish to serve the bread warm, reheat in the oven at 340°F (170°C/Gas Mark 3) for 8 minutes.

7oz (200g) bakers flour, type 55
10½oz (300g) all-purpose/plain flour—
wholemeal or brown
⅔oz (20g) yeast, fresh
10¼fl oz (310ml) water, cold
⅓fl oz (10ml) olive oil
⅓oz (10g) table salt
softened butter for greasing
flour for dusting

EQUIPMENT
Electric mixer and hook attachment
2 bread loaf tins, 10in (25cm) x 3¾in (9cm)
x 3¼in (8cm) deep
2 mixing bowls, 4in (10cm) diameter
Baking paper
Pastry brush
Plastic wrap

TIPS AND TRICKS
You can use this recipe to make fruit bread to be served with cheese. Just add 2oz (60g) chopped walnuts, 1½oz (40g) dried apricots and 1½oz (40g) sultanas in Step 1.
This recipe can also be used to make a brown bread version of Mini White Baguettes (see recipe).

Bread Dough

FETA & BUTTERMILK BREAD ROLLS

Petit Pain au Feta

MAKES 18

This is a beautiful bread that is ideal for serving at a dinner party to impress your guests.

17½oz (500g) bakers flour, type 55

¾oz (25g) yeast, fresh

4fl oz (125ml) water, cold

⅓fl oz (10ml) olive oil

5fl oz (150ml) buttermilk

⅔oz (20g) unsalted butter, softened

½oz (15g) table salt

¾oz (25g) superfine/caster sugar

⅓oz (10g) sea salt

7fl oz (200ml) water, cold

7oz (200g) feta cheese

Extra olive oil, for drizzling

EQUIPMENT

Electric mixer and hook attachment

Knife

2 mixing bowls, 4in (10cm) diameter

2 baking trays

Baking paper

Pastry brush

Plastic wrap

TIPS AND TRICKS

For more flavour, add chopped herbs or sundried tomato with the feta.

Substitute the feta with any cheese of your choice.

1. PREPARE THE BREAD DOUGH

Place the flour, fresh yeast, water, oil, buttermilk and butter into the bowl of an electric mixer.

Using the hook attachment, mix the dough on a slow speed then build up to medium speed. Let the dough turn for 6 minutes, then add salt and sugar, then let it turn for a further 4 minutes.

Stop the machine, remove the dough and place into a bowl. Wrap with plastic wrap and set aside at room temperature to rise for 20 minutes.

2. PROVE THE DOUGH

After the dough has rested, take the dough and roll by hand to a length of 8in (20cm) length, then cut in half lengthways, then into 18 pieces. Turn each piece onto its side.

Line 2 baking trays with baking paper, and place rolls on the trays. Preheat the oven to 110°F (50°C/Gas Mark ¼) and when it reaches that temperature turn it off. Place both trays inside to allow the bread to rise, about 20 minutes. Remove the trays from the oven and set aside.

In a bowl dissolve the salt in the water. Brush the rolls with salted water and, using three fingers, press indentations into each piece. Fill the cavities with chunks of feta.

3. BAKE AND SERVE

Preheat the oven to 345°F (175°C/Gas Mark 4) and bake for 15 minutes. Drizzle olive oil over the rolls before serving. Serve immediately while warm.

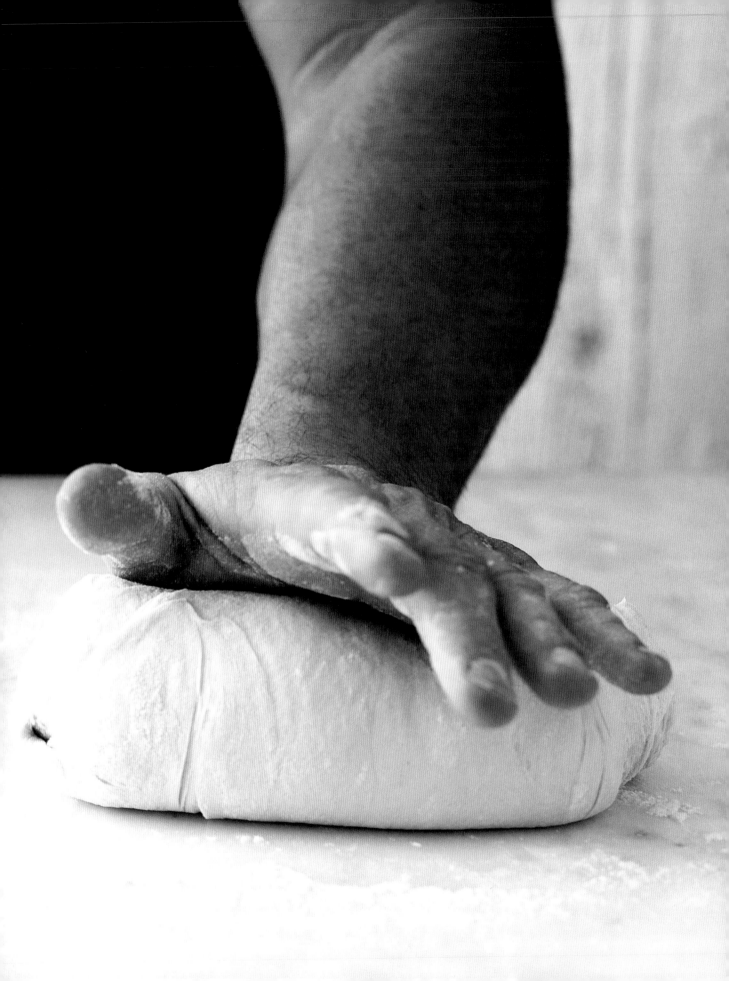

FLAT BREAD
Focaccia

Makes 1 slab

Focaccia is most widely identified with the region of Liguria in Italy. It is a flat, oven-baked bread, with a spongier, less crunchy texture than traditional breads and it can also have a variety of toppings.

1. Prepare the bread dough

Place the flour, fresh yeast, water and olive oil into the bowl of an electric mixer with hook attachment, mix the dough on a slow speed then build up to medium speed for 6 minutes. Add the salt and continue turning for 4 minutes

2. Prove the dough

Preheat the oven to 110°F (50°C/Gas Mark ¼) and when it reaches that temperature turn it off. After the dough has rested for 20 minutes and risen, roll it into an 8in (20cm) x 12in (30cm) rectangle using a rolling pin. Place it on a baking tray lined with baking paper and place tray inside to allow the bread to rise, for an additional 20–30 minutes. Remove from the oven and place on the kitchen bench. Brush the top of the proven dough with ⅔fl oz (20ml) of olive oil. Push your fingertips into the dough to create dimples on the surface. Drizzle a little more olive oil and scatter with sea salt, rosemary and thyme.

3. Bake and serve

Preheat the oven to 345°F (175°C/Gas Mark 4). Bake focaccia for 20–25 minutes until light golden in colour. Serve warm or at room temperature. Baked focaccia can be frozen, wrapped in plastic wrap, for up to 1 month.

Makes 30oz (860g)

17½oz (500g) bakers flour, type 55

1oz (30g) yeast, fresh

10½fl oz (300ml) water

1¾fl oz (50ml) olive oil

⅓oz (10g) table salt

1¾fl oz (50ml) olive oil, extra

⅓oz (10g) sea salt, for topping

2 sprigs fresh rosemary, chopped

2 sprigs fresh thyme, chopped

EQUIPMENT

Electric mixer and hook attachment

Knife

Rolling pin

Baking tray

Baking paper

Pastry brush

PIZZA DOUGH FOR A CLASSIC PIZZA

Pâte à Pizza

MAKES 25OZ (720G)—TWO 12IN (30CM) DIAMETER PIZZAS

The word pizza comes from the Latin verb 'pinsere' which means to press and it originates from Naples.

Makes 25oz (720g)

8fl oz (240ml) water

1/6oz (6g) yeast, fresh

1/8oz (3g) superfine/caster sugar

15½oz (440g) all-purpose/plain flour

1/8oz (3g) salt

1fl oz (30ml) olive oil

oil for spraying

flour for dusting

9oz (250g) Tomato Base Sauce

Topping of your choice

TOMATO BASE SAUCE

Makes 14oz (400g)

1fl oz (30oz) vegetable oil

½ brown onion, finely diced

3 cloves garlic, finely diced

2 sprigs fresh thyme, finely chopped

2 sprigs fresh rosemary, finely chopped

3 pinches brown sugar

2 teaspoons tomato paste/puree

5 Roma tomatoes, roughly diced

1 x 15oz (450g) can whole tomatoes in juice,
    diced

1. PREPARE THE PIZZA DOUGH

Warm the water slightly and dissolve the yeast, sugar and 1½oz (40g) of the flour; whisk until combined. Cover the bowl with plastic wrap and leave in a warm place for 10 minutes.

Meanwhile, place 14oz (400g) of flour, salt, olive oil and the yeast mix in the bowl of an electric mixer with hook attachment. Mix for 8 minutes on a low speed. Cover the bowl in plastic wrap, leave to rest in a warm place and allow dough to rise for 20 minutes.

Lightly flour a bench top. Using your knuckles, knock the air out of the dough. Separate the dough into 2 portions (this will give you 2 bases)—10½oz (300g) for a thin base or 12oz (350g) for a thicker base. Lightly spray each pizza tray with oil and dust with flour. Using a rolling pin, roll each dough to 12in (30cm) in diameter, then place the dough onto the pizza tray. Push the dough with your fingertips to the very edge of the tray. Using the fork, prick the surface of the base lightly. Cover with plastic wrap and refrigerate until needed, for no more than 4 hours.

2. PREPARE THE TOMATO BASE SAUCE

Place the saucepan over a medium to high heat and add the vegetable oil. Slowly cook the onion, garlic and herbs until the onions are translucent (about 5 minutes), stirring occasionally. Stir in the brown sugar and the tomato paste and cook for 1 minute. Stir in the fresh tomatoes, canned tomatoes with liquid and basil, then bring to the boil. Reduce the heat to low and simmer for about 30 minutes, stirring occasionally. At the end of cooking, there still should be a little liquid left in the sauce. Season with salt and pepper. Cool before use.

3. Assemble, bake and serve

Preheat the oven to 350°F (180°C/Gas Mark 4). Spread 9oz (250g) of tomato base sauce onto each pizza and add the topping of your choice. Bake the pizzas for 10 minutes, then slide off the tray onto a rack. Cook for a further 8 minutes until the edges are lightly coloured.

Topping ideas

There any many choices for toppings including vegetables, cured meats and seafood—go crazy experimenting.

3 fresh basil leaves, finely chopped

Salt and pepper to taste

EQUIPMENT

Electric mixer with hook attachment

2 pizza trays, 12in (30cm) diameter

Saucepan, 8in (20cm) diameter

Wooden spoon

Whisk

Rolling pin

Plastic wrap

Fork

Knife

TIPS AND TRICKS

It is best to use fresh yeast to get a superior quality dough.

When rolling, don't be afraid to use a lot of flour so the dough doesn't stick.

Oven trays can be substituted for pizza trays.

Bread dough

CHOCOLATE PIZZA
Pizza au Chocolat

Makes one 12in (30cm) pizza, to serve 6

This is a simple recipe using everyone's favourite ingredient—chocolate.

3½ oz (100g) Crème Pâtissière (see
   Vanilla Slice)

½ quantity 12½oz (360g) Pizza Dough
   (see recipe)

7oz (200g) chocolate, roughly chopped—dark,
   milk or white

2 bananas, sliced

1 mango, peeled and thinly sliced

1¾oz (50g) red grapes

fresh mint leaves

1¾oz (50g) roasted hazelnuts

EQUIPMENT

Pizza tray, 12in (30cm) diameter

Knife

TIPS AND TRICKS

You can add your favourite chocolate lollies on
   top for variety.

1. Prepare the pizza base
Make the pizza base (see recipe). Spread the crème pâtissière on the pizza base as you would a tomato sauce.

2. Assemble, bake and serve
Preheat the oven to 350°F (180°C/Gas Mark 4). Bake the pizza base for about 20 minutes until lightly golden. Sprinkle chocolate on top of the crème pâtissière, scatter the sliced banana, mango, grapes, mint leaves and hazelnut and slide the pizza base off the tray onto a rack in the oven. Bake for a further 2–3 minutes until the edges of the pizza base are lightly golden.

PASSIONFRUIT AND MANGO CALZONE

Fruit de la Passion et Mangue Calzone

MAKES 1 CALZONE, TO SERVE 3

Calzone is a folded or half-moon shaped pizza—it can be filled with sweet or savoury ingredients.

1. PREPARE THE PIZZA BASE

Make the pizza base following the recipe. Lightly flour the bench top and, using a rolling pin, roll the pizza base into a 12in (30cm) x 9in (22cm) oval. Place the dough on a baking tray lined with baking paper.

2. ASSEMBLE, BAKE AND SERVE

Preheat the oven to 350°F (180°C/Gas Mark 4). Place the crème pâtissière into the bowl and whisk to a smooth consistency. Brush egg wash around the edge of the oval and place the crème pâtissière on one half of the oval, leave a 1/8in (1/2cm) gap to close the calzone. Place the sliced mango evenly on top of the crème pâtissière then top with the passionfruit. Fold the other half of the dough on top, in half, and gently seal by pinching the edges with your forefinger and thumb, to fully seal the calzone. Brush egg wash over the top and sprinkle with raw sugar. Bake for 20–25 minutes until lightly golden. Remove from the oven and dust with confectioner's sugar—the calzone can be served warm.

1 quantity 25oz (720g) Pizza Dough (see recipe)

3½ oz (100g) Crème Pâtissière (see Vanilla Slice)

1 egg for egg wash

2 mangoes, flesh only, sliced

2 passionfruits

1oz (30g) raw sugar

3½ oz (100g) confectioner's/icing sugar for dusting

EQUIPMENT

Pastry brush

Knife

Whisk

Rolling pin

Baking tray

Baking paper

Plastic wrap

Brioche Dough

Pâte à Brioche

BRIOCHE DOUGH
Pâte à Brioche

MAKES 60OZ (1.7KG)

Brioche is made in a similar way to bread; however, with the addition of eggs and butter it is considered a pastry. It is believed to have originated in Normandy in northern France around 1404. The name comes from the verb 'brier', which means 'to work the dough with a wooden roller, which is called a "broye" or "brie" '.

24oz (675g) bakers flour

8 eggs (1¾–2oz/50–55g each)

4fl oz (125ml) milk, warm

²/3oz (20g) salt

4oz (120g) superfine/caster sugar

1oz (30g) yeast, fresh

14oz (400g) unsalted butter, softened

EQUIPMENT
Electric mixer with hook attachment

Baking tray, standard size

Plastic wrap

TIPS AND TRICKS
Fresh yeast is best for this recipe, rather than dried yeast. As the dough is 'alive' with fresh yeast, it will only keep for a maximum of 2 days.

Do not let the fresh yeast sit in direct contact with sugar or salt as this will kill the yeast.

When raising the dough (also known as proving), it is best to do this in a preheated oven at 110°F (50°C/Gas

1. Place all ingredients except the butter in the bowl of an electric mixer with hook attachment—the hook attachment helps develop the gluten in the dough, which is important for all breads. Mix the dough on low speed until all combined, then increase to full speed and mix until the dough comes together and starts to slap against the side of the bowl. This should take around 8 minutes at full speed—you may need to hold the mixer as it can move around.

2. Add the softened butter and mix again on full speed until all the butter is incorporated—at this point you may need to scrape down the sides of the bowl to ensure you incorporate all the butter. The dough should be smooth, glossy and elastic.

3. Flour the baking tray, place the dough on top and sprinkle flour on the top of the dough. Place plastic wrap in direct contact with the surface of the dough. Rest the dough in the refrigerator overnight before using. This dough can be kept in the refrigerator for 2 days maximum.

Mark ¼) (for loaves) and 100°F (40°C/Gas Mark ¼) (for smaller brioche) that has been turned off. The ideal temperature to prove brioche is 90–100°F (35–40°C/Gas Mark ¼). A covered warm place will raise the dough, but it will take longer than if using the oven.

You can add fruit or nuts to the dough before proving if you would like variations on this recipe.

BRIOCHE LOAF
Brioche

Brioche is a such a versatile dough—it can be used for breakfast, lunch or dinner. The ultimate is to serve it toasted with foie gras.

21oz (600g) Brioche dough (see recipe)

1¾oz (50g) flour for dusting

oil for spraying

EQUIPMENT

Bread loaf tin, 10in (25cm) x 3¾in (9cm)
*   x 3¼in (8cm) deep*

Baking paper

Cooling rack

TIPS AND TRICKS

A great variation to this recipe is the addition of 8½oz (240g) red praline (almonds coated with red sugar) added 2 minutes before the dough has stopped turning.

1. PREPARE THE BRIOCHE DOUGH

Preheat the oven to 110°F (50°C/Gas Mark ¼) then turn it off once it has reached that temperature. Spray the loaf tin with oil and line with baking paper. Lightly dust the bench top with flour. Roll the brioche dough into a baton shape about 9in (22cm) long and place the baton, smoothest side facing up for presentation, in a loaf tin. Place the loaf tin in the oven, turned off, and let the dough rise for 40–60 minutes, or until it doubles in size. Remove the loaf tin from the oven.

2. BAKE AND SERVE

Preheat the oven to 340°F (170°C/Gas Mark 3). Bake the loaf for 25 minutes, turning around halfway through cooking. Remove the loaf tin from the oven and unmould the brioche onto a cooling rack. Tap the side of the loaf—if it sounds hollow, then the loaf is ready. If not, put the loaf back in the tin in the oven to cook further. Best served within 4 hours.

SUGARED BRIOCHE
Brioche au Sucre

MAKES 6 TO 8 INDIVIDUAL

Children will love this recipe—it's simple and tastes great without being too sweet.

1. PREPARE THE BRIOCHE DOUGH

Preheat the oven to 100°F (40°C/Gas Mark ¼) then turn it off once it has reached that temperature. Lightly flour the bench top and the moulds. Roll the brioche dough flat into a circle approximately ½in (1cm) thick. Use the cutter to cut 10 discs of dough, about ¾oz (25g) each. Place a dough disc in each mould then place in the oven, turned off, for 20 minutes to rise. Once the discs have risen, remove tray from the oven, egg wash the top of the discs and sprinkle the sugar on top.

2. BAKE AND SERVE

Preheat the oven to 340°F (170°C/Gas Mark 3). Bake the brioche for 15–20 minutes until golden brown, turning the tray around halfway through cooking. Remove the brioche from the moulds then serve immediately.

3½ oz (100g) flour for dusting

9oz (250g) Brioche dough (see recipe)

1 egg for egg wash

3½ oz (100g) superfine/caster sugar, pearl sugar or raw sugar

EQUIPMENT

Rolling pin

Cutter round, 2in (5cm)

8 tartlet moulds, round, 2½in (6cm) x ¾in (2cm)

Baking tray

Pastry brush

BRIOCHE BUNS
Chichi à la Crème

MAKES 10

Chichi are the French version of a doughnut—deep fried pastry.

softened butter for greasing

flour for dusting

17½oz (500g) Brioche dough (see recipe)

48fl oz (1.5L) vegetable oil for frying

3½ oz (100g) superfine/caster sugar

½ teaspoon cinnamon

7oz (200g) Crème Pâtissière (see Vanilla Slice)

EQUIPMENT

Rolling pin

10 tart moulds, round, 3¾in (9cm) x ¾in (2cm)

Cutter, round, 2¾in (7cm)

Saucepan, 9in (22cm) diameter

Slotted spoon

Paper towel

Mixing bowl, 9in (22cm)

Baking tray

Wooden stick (pencil thickness)

Piping bag

Piping nozzle no. 804

TIPS AND TRICKS

You can vary the fillings—use a jelly/jam, flavoured crème pâtissière, rhubarb or apple compote.

Make sure the oil maintains the same temperature throughout cooking.

1. PREPARE THE BRIOCHE DOUGH

Preheat the oven to 100°F (40°C/Gas Mark ¼) then turn it off once it has reached that temperature. Butter and flour each of the moulds. Lightly flour the bench top. Roll the brioche dough flat into a circle approximately ½in (1cm) thick. Use the cutter to cut 10 discs of dough—about 1¾–2oz (50–60g) each. Place the discs in 10 moulds on a baking tray in the oven, turned off, for 20 minutes to rise. Once the brioche have risen, remove tray from the oven and set aside on the bench top.

2. COOK AND SERVE

Place the oil in the saucepan—there should be at least 2½in (6cm) of oil. Heat over a high heat to a temperature of 340–350°F (175–180°C/Gas Mark 4). Have the slotted spoon and paper towel on a plate next to the pan. Remove a bun from a mould and gently slide into the oil—cook 4 buns at a time in this sized pan (do not overcrowd the pan too much). Cook the buns for 4 minutes then turn them over. Cook for a further 1 minute—they should be golden brown in colour. Using the slotted spoon, remove from the oil then place on the paper towel to drain. Repeat until all the buns are cooked.

In a bowl, place the sugar and cinnamon, and mix well. Toss the cooked buns in the sugar to coat. With the wooden stick, make a hole in the side of the bun and make a cavity in the middle by twisting the wooden stick. Place the crème pâtissière in the piping bag with nozzle no. 804 and pipe into each bun until full, about ⅔oz (20g) in each. Serve immediately.

SCONES

Scones

MAKES 6

As the name suggests, scones are Scottish in origin and were in the past made with unleavened oats and cooked on a griddle. Today they often feature on high-tea menus and there are many variations in flavour, both sweet and savoury.

9oz (250g) all-purpose/plain flour

2¼oz (65g) superfine/caster sugar

½oz (15g) baking powder

Pinch salt

2¼oz (65g) unsalted butter, diced and cold

2¾fl oz (100ml) buttermilk

1¾fl oz (50ml) milk for milk wash

flour for dusting

EQUIPMENT

Mixing bowl, 9in (22cm) diameter

Rolling pin

Cutter, round, 2½in (6cm)

Baking tray

Baking paper

Pastry brush

TIPS AND TRICKS

Flavour variations for the dough can include dried fruit, sultanas or dates. Savoury scones can include spinach and feta, bacon and cheese, or baked pumpkin.

Dough can be stored in the refrigerator for up to 2 days before baking.

1. PREPARE THE DOUGH

Place the flour, sugar, baking powder, salt and butter in a bowl. Rub the ingredients between your hands so that a sandy consistency is achieved. Add buttermilk and mix with one hand until everything is combined into a rough dough. Lightly flour the bench top and roll the brioche dough flat into a circle approximately 1in (2.5cm) thick. The thickness of the dough is important to ensure that the scones have enough height.

2. ASSEMBLE, BAKE AND SERVE

Preheat the oven to 340°F (170°C/Gas Mark 3). Cut out the scones with a 2½in (6cm) cutter and turn them upside down onto a baking tray lined with baking paper. Press the remaining dough together, roll it out again and cut out more scones—you should have 6 in total. Lightly brush a little milk on top of the scone, twice, sprinkle the top of each scone with flour to create a rustic effect. Bake scones for 15–20 minutes until lightly golden. Scones are classically served with jam and whipped cream. Best consumed within 4 hours.

CLASSIC DOUGHNUTS MADE FROM BRIOCHE

Brioche Doughnuts

MAKES 10

1. PREPARE THE BRIOCHE DOUGH

Preheat the oven to 100°F (40°C/Gas Mark ¼) then turn it off once it has reached that temperature. Butter and flour each of the moulds. Lightly flour the bench top. Roll the brioche dough flat into a circle approximately ⅔in (1.5cm) thick. Use the cutter to cut 10 discs of dough, about 2¼oz (70g) each. Using the smaller cutter, cut a hole in the centre of each disc. Place the moulds on a baking tray in the oven, turned off, for 20 minutes to rise. Once the doughnuts have risen, remove tray from the oven and set aside on the bench top.

2. TO COOK AND SERVE

Place the oil in the saucepan—there should be at least 2½in (6cm) of oil. Heat over a high heat to a temperature of 340–350°F (175–180°C/Gas Mark 4). Have the slotted spoon and paper towel on a plate next to the pan. Remove a doughnut from a mould and gently slide into the oil—cook 4 doughnuts at a time in this sized pan (do not overcrowd the pan too much). Cook the doughnuts for 1 minute then turn them over and cook for a further 1 minute. Using a slotted spoon, remove from the oil and place on the paper towels to drain. Repeat until all doughnuts are cooked.

Whisk the jelly to remove any lumps. Lightly brush some jelly on the top of each doughnut and then dip the doughnut, jelly side down, into the sprinkles.

21oz (600g) Brioche dough (see recipe)
softened butter for greasing
flour for dusting
48fl oz (1.5L) vegetable oil for frying
3½ oz (100g) jelly/jam
3½ oz (100g) sprinkles

EQUIPMENT
Rolling pin
10 tart moulds, round, 3¾in (9cm) x ¾in (2cm)
Cutter, 3¼in (8cm)
Cutter, 1¼in (3cm)
Saucepan, 9in (22cm) diameter
Slotted spoon
Paper towels
Baking tray
Mixing bowl, 8in (20cm) diameter
Whisk

CHOCOLATE TIE
Cravate au chocolat

MAKES 12

This is an ideal treat for morning tea for the children.

21oz (600g) Brioche dough (see recipe)

flour for dusting

1 egg for egg wash

3½ oz (100g) chocolate chips (or chopped chocolate), white, milk or dark

1¾oz (50g) confectioner's/icing sugar

EQUIPMENT

Rolling pin

Knife

Pastry brush

Baking tray

Baking paper

1. PREPARE THE BRIOCHE DOUGH
Preheat the oven to 110°F (50°C/Gas Mark ¼) then turn it off once it has reached that temperature. Lightly flour the bench top. Using a rolling pin, roll the brioche dough into a 16in (40cm) square about ¼in (5mm) thick. Very lightly egg wash one half of the dough, then sprinkle the chocolate chips on top of the egg wash. Fold the other half of the dough on top of the chocolate chips and lightly press the dough down. Cut the rectangle into 12 strips, each about 1¼in (3cm) wide. Place the strips on a baking tray lined with baking paper in the oven, turned off, for 20 minutes to rise. Once the strips have risen, remove tray from the oven and set aside on the bench top.

2. BAKE AND SERVE
Preheat the oven to 340°F (170°C/Gas Mark 3). Brush egg wash on the top of the strips and bake for 12–15 minutes until light golden. Remove from the oven and cool. Dust with sugar and serve immediately.

ST TROPEZ SPECIALITY
Tarte Tropézienne

MAKES 8 TO 10

A Polish pastry chef, Alexandre Micka settled into St Tropez and in the 1950s invented the tarte Tropézienne. He was on the filmset of the Brigitte Bardot movie And God Created Woman *and she was the one who named this delicious pastry.*

1. PREPARE THE BRIOCHE DOUGH

Preheat the oven to 110°F (50°C/Gas Mark ¼) then turn it off once it has reached that temperature. Butter and flour each of the moulds. Lightly flour the bench top. Roll the brioche dough flat into a circle approximately ⅔in (1.5cm) thick. Use the cutter to cut 10 discs of dough, about 2¼oz (70g) each and place into the prepared moulds. Place the moulds on a baking tray in the oven, turned off, for 20 minutes to rise. Once the dough has risen, remove the tray from the oven and set aside on the bench top. Preheat the oven to 340°F (170°C/Gas Mark 3). Brush egg wash over the top of the brioche and sprinkle some sugar on top of each. Bake for 18–25 minutes until light golden. Remove the brioche from the moulds and allow to cool.

2. PREPARE THE TROPÉZIENNE PUNCH

Place the water and sugar in a saucepan and boil over a high heat. Remove pan from the heat and stir in the rum; set aside at room temperature.

3. ASSEMBLE AND SERVE

Cut each of the brioche in half horizontally with the serrated knife. Brush the insides of both the base and lid with the sugar syrup. Place the crème pâtissière in a bowl and whisk to a smooth consistency. Pour into a piping bag with nozzle no. 804 and pipe a spiral to completely cover the base (about 1½oz/40g each) then place the lid back on top. Serve immediately.

25oz (700g) Brioche dough (see recipe)

softened butter for greasing

flour for dusting

3½ oz (100g) pearl sugar, superfine/caster sugar or raw sugar

14oz (400g) Crème Pâtissière (see Vanilla Slice)

1 egg for eggwash

TROPÉZIENNE PUNCH

8fl oz (250ml) water

4oz (125g) superfine/caster sugar

⅔fl oz (20ml) rum

EQUIPMENT

Rolling pin

Cutter, round, 3¼in (8cm)

10 tart moulds, round, 3¾in (9cm) x ¾in (2cm)

Baking tray

2 pastry brushes

Serrated knife

Bowl, 9in (22cm) diameter

Whisk

Piping bag

Piping nozzle no. 804

Saucepan, 8in (20cm) diameter

Flexible spatula

Brioche Dough

SUMMER FRUIT PUDDING
Pudding aux Fruits Rouges

MAKES 4

This seasonal dessert of brioche and berries is said to be of British origin. It gained popularity in the late nineteenth and early twentieth centuries.

36oz (1kg) mixed berries, frozen

2oz (60g) confectioner's/icing sugar

1 punnet fresh strawberries

1 punnet fresh blueberries

1 punnet fresh raspberries

½fl oz (15ml) Grand Marnier

1 baked Brioche Loaf (see recipe)

1. PREPARE THE BERRIES

In the saucepan, heat the frozen berries and 1¾oz (50g) of the sugar over a medium heat until all the berries are broken down. Blend in a food processor until it turns to liquid. Pass through the sieve (see Glossary) into a bowl to remove any seeds or lumps, then set aside the berry coulis.

Remove any stems or leaves from the fresh berries and roughly chop into ½–⅔in (1–1.5cm) chunks. Place the chopped berries in a bowl and sprinkle with the remaining sugar and Grand Marnier. Toss the berries to distribute the sugar and liquor, then leave to rest at room temperature.

2. ASSEMBLE AND SERVE

Trim the crust off the whole loaf using the serrated knife—be careful to cut as little of the white centre as possible. Turn the loaf on its side and cut into 8 slices lengthways (about ½in/1cm thick, depending on the size of the loaf). Take 4 slices and cut 8 discs of bread using the round cutter—2 per slice. Trim the other 4 slices to the height of the cake ring (2in/5cm) to form strips. Place the 4 cake rings on a baking tray that can fit in the refrigerator. Take 4 circles of brioche, dip each into the blended coulis and soak. Place 1 soaked circle of brioche in the bottom of each cake ring. Then take 1 strip of brioche and soak it in the

coulis. Place the strip around the inside of the ring. Repeat for each strip. Generously fill the centre of the pudding with the fresh berries. Soak the remaining circles in the coulis and place them on top of each of the puddings, pressing down firmly.

Set them in the refrigerator for 2 hours—place a tray on top of the puddings to weigh them down. To serve, place the puddings in their moulds on the plate, then gently slide the ring off. Serve with the remaining coulis, berries and good quality vanilla ice cream.

EQUIPMENT

Saucepan, 8in (20cm) diameter

Wooden spoon

Food processor

Sieve

2 mixing bowls, 8in (20cm) diameter

Knife

Serrated knife

Chopping board

Cutter, round, 2½in (6cm)

4 cake rings, 3in (7.5cm) diameter x 2in
  (5cm) deep

TIPS AND TRICKS

It is preferable to make this pudding 24 hours before serving as the flavour will intensify.

Seasonal fruit such as mango, cherries or plums can be substituted for the fresh berries.

Brioche Dough

KOUGLOF

In France it's kouglof, in Germany it's gugelhupf—whatever you may call it, this brioche-style cake made with sultanas and almonds is delicious.

2¼oz (70g) sultanas

2¼oz (70g) almonds, whole and unblanched

3½ oz (100g) confectioner's/icing sugar to dust

21oz (600g) Brioche dough (see recipe)

softened butter for greasing

flour for dusting

EQUIPMENT

Electric mixer with hook attachment

Mould, kouglof, 9in (22cm) diameter

1. PREPARE THE BRIOCHE DOUGH

After you have completed the first 3 steps in the recipe for Brioche Dough, add the sultanas and almonds then mix again on full speed for 2 minutes or until well combined—the dough should be smooth, glossy and elastic. Preheat the oven to 110°F (50°C/Gas Mark ¼) then turn it off once it has reached that temperature. Butter and flour the kouglof mould. On a floured bench top, use your hands to roll the dough into a log approximately 12in (30cm) long and place the log into the kouglof mould. Place the kouglof in the oven, turned off, and let it rise until doubled in size. Remove the kouglof mould from the oven.

2. BAKE AND SERVE

Preheat the oven to 340°F (170°C/Gas Mark 3). Bake the kouglof for 25 minutes. Remove from the oven, allow to cool slightly before removing the mould and dust the kouglof with sugar. Serve immediately at room temperature.

FRENCH TOAST
Pain Perdu

SERVES 5 (2 SLICES PER SERVE)

Pain perdu means 'lost bread' and is a great way to use leftover bread—it can be served as a dessert as well as breakfast. In this recipe we use brioche, which gives it a wonderful flavour.

1. TO MAKE TOAST

Place the eggs, sugar, milk, vanilla and cinnamon in a bowl, and whisk to combine. Slice the brioche loaf into 1in (2.5cm) slices—about 10 slices per loaf. Heat the frying pan with 1/3oz (10g) butter over a medium to high heat. While the pan is heating, soak 2 slices of bread thoroughly in the egg mixture, for about 30 seconds each side. Once the butter is bubbling, place the soaked slices in the pan and cook each side of the slice until lightly coloured—about 1 minute each side. Repeat to cook all the brioche, putting 1/3oz (10g) butter in the pan between batches. Serve immediately on a plate with seasonal fruit and maple syrup.

10 eggs (1¾–2oz/50–55g each)

5oz (150g) superfine/caster sugar

16fl oz (500ml) milk

5 teaspoons vanilla essence

10 pinches cinnamon

1 baked Brioche Loaf (see recipe)

1½oz (40g) unsalted butter

EQUIPMENT

Serrated knife

Frying pan, 12in (30cm) diameter

Chopping board

Whisk

Flexible spatula

Mixing bowl, 8in (20cm)

TIPS AND TRICKS

If you like spice, substitute the brioche loaf with a loaf of Gingerbread (see recipe).

Brioche Dough

SAVARIN

Savarin

MAKES 1 ROUND TO SERVE 10 PEOPLE

The original baba was introduced to France by King Stanislas, who was exiled from Poland. Many years later in 1844, two Parisian brothers, the Julien brothers, were inspired by the rum baba and created the savarin.

21oz (600g) Brioche dough (see recipe)

softened butter for greasing

flour for dusting

3 quantities Tropézienne Punch syrup
  (see St Tropez Speciality), warm

10½oz (300g) Crème Chantilly (see Croissant
  Basket with Berries)

10½oz (300g) seasonal fruit

EQUIPMENT

Savarin mould, 9in (22cm) round

Saucepan, 8in (20cm) diameter

Baking tray, deep

Cake rack

2 cake lifters or large palette knife

TIPS AND TRICKS

Once the savarin is baked, it should be soaked
  in the syrup within 4 hours.

1. PREPARE THE SAVARIN

Preheat the oven to 110°F (50°C/Gas Mark ¼) then turn it off once it has reached that temperature. Butter and flour the savarin mould. Lightly flour a bench top. Roll the dough by hand to an 18in (45cm) log and place around the mould. Place the savarin mould in the oven, turned off, and let rise until it has doubled in size—about 1 hour. Remove the savarin mould from the oven.

Reheat the oven to 340°F (170°C/Gas Mark 3). Bake the savarin for 12–15 minutes. Remove from the oven and let it cool on a cake rack. Remove savarin from mould.

2. ASSEMBLE AND SERVE

Place the cake rack on a deep baking tray and pour the warm syrup over the savarin. Remove the rack and pour the excess syrup back into the saucepan; repeat the soaking process 3 more times or until the savarin is moist and spongy. Using the cake lifters, lift the savarin onto a serving plate. Fill the centre of the savarin with crème chantilly and top with fruit. Serve immediately.

HOT CROSS BUNS

Hot Cross Buns

MAKES 10

Hot cross buns are traditionally eaten at Easter and the cross is said to represent the crucifixion of Jesus Christ.

DOUGH

7fl oz (200ml) milk, warm

1¾oz (50g) yeast, fresh

12oz (350g) all-purpose/plain flour

¾oz (25g) unsalted butter

1¾oz (50g) superfine/caster sugar

¼oz (8g) milk powder

2oz (60g) currants

¾oz (25g) sultanas

¾oz (25g) mixed peel

softened butter for greasing

flour for dusting

3½ oz (100g) apricot jelly/jam for glazing

PIPING PASTE

2¼oz (65g) all-purpose/plain flour

2½fl oz (80ml) water

¼oz (8g) superfine/caster sugar

1. PREPARE THE DOUGH

In a bowl, whisk together the milk and yeast, then set aside in a warm place for 10 minutes. Place all the other dough ingredients in the bowl of an electric mixer with a hook attachment, and mix on medium speed. Add the milk and yeast mixture then mix the dough for about 4 minutes. Remove the bowl from the mixer and cover it with plastic wrap—leave in a warm place for about 1 hour.

Preheat the oven to 110°F (50°C/Gas Mark ¼) then turn it off once it has reached that temperature. Butter and flour the cake tin. Lightly flour a bench top. Using a rolling pin, roll the dough into a 20in (50cm) long log. Cut the log into 10 portions, about 2½oz (80g) each. Arrange the 10 portions in the cake tin, wrap in plastic wrap, place in the oven, turned off, and allow to rise for 1 hour.

2. PIPING PASTE

Mix all the ingredients in a bowl until a paste is formed. Add more water if required to ensure a thick, pipeable consistency.

3. Bake and serve

Preheat the oven to 340°F (170°C/Gas Mark 3). Place the sugar for crosses in a piping bag with nozzle no. 801 and pipe a cross on the top of each bun. Bake for 25–30 minutes. Remove from the oven and while the buns are still hot, glaze the tops with apricot jelly for shine. Best served warm with butter. Store buns in an airtight container, once cooled, for up to 3 days.

EQUIPMENT

Electric mixer with hook attachment

Mixing bowl, 8in (20cm)

Plastic wrap

Rolling pin

Cake tin, 9½in (24cm) diameter

Whisk

Wooden spoon

Piping bag

Piping nozzle no. 801

Pastry brush

Gingerbread

Pain d'Épices

GINGERBREAD LOAF
Pain d'Épices

MAKES 2 LOAVES

This is a spice bread often referred to as gingerbread, which originated in Reims in the Champagne-Ardennes region; however, now Dijon claims this famous bread.

6½fl oz (190ml) milk

2 cinnamon sticks

grated zest of 1 orange

3 cloves

2 star anise

5 coriander seeds

5 whole eggs (1¾–2oz/50–55g each)

2½ oz (75g) superfine/caster sugar

6½oz (190g) all-purpose/plain flour

1oz (30g) baking powder

1/6oz (6g) mixed spice

4 pinches grated nutmeg

6½oz (190g) honey

softened butter for greasing

EQUIPMENT

Mixing bowl, 8in (20cm) diameter

Flexible spatula

2 loaf tins, 10in (25cm) x 3¾in (9cm) x
   3¼in (8cm) deep

Baking paper

Saucepan, 8in (20cm)

Whisk

Sieve

Pastry brush

Baking tray

Cake rack

1. PREPARE THE GINGERBREAD MIXTURE

Place the milk, cinnamon sticks, orange zest, cloves, star anise and coriander seeds into a saucepan over a medium heat and bring to the boil. When the first bubbles appear, remove from heat and set aside to cool in the refrigerator. Whisk the eggs and sugar together in a mixing bowl until they are well combined, then add the dry ingredients and follow with the honey. Strain the milk into a bowl (see Glossary), add to the gingerbread mixture and stir until well combined.

2. BAKE AND SERVE

Preheat the oven to 300°F (150°C/Gas Mark 2). Butter the inside of each loaf tin and line with baking paper. Place half the mixture into each tin. Bake for 50 minutes. Remove from oven and unmould onto a cake rack. Lightly brush the top of each loaf with honey to create a glossy effect. This bread can be kept at room temperature, wrapped in plastic wrap, for 3 days. It can be kept in the freezer for 1 month.

The best way to enjoy this loaf is to serve it warm, with butter.

Gingerbread

GINGERBREAD PEOPLE

Gingerbread People

MAKES 10

All the little ones love gingerbread, especially with lots of colours and patterns. This recipe is dedicated to Tom, James, Charlie, Emily, Chloe and William—Michelle's nieces and nephews—who never say no to a gingerbread treat.

Makes 43oz (1.3kg)

7oz (200g) unsalted butter, softened

5½oz (160g) brown sugar

21oz (600g) all-purpose/plain flour

1 whole egg (1¾–2oz/50–55g)

1 egg yolk

2½oz (80g) molasses

2½oz (80g) honey

¼oz (8g) baking soda/bicarbonate of soda

¼oz (8g) all spice

1oz (30g) ground ginger

EQUIPMENT

Electric mixer with paddle attachment

Rolling pin

Baking tray

Baking paper

Plastic wrap

Cutters, people shaped

TIPS AND TRICKS

To make royal icing—see recipe for Gingerbread House.

1. PREPARE THE GINGERBREAD DOUGH

Place the softened butter and sugar into the bowl of an electric mixer with paddle attachment. Mix on medium speed until the mixture starts to lighten in colour. Add the flour, egg, egg yolk, molasses, honey, baking soda, all spice and ground ginger and mix until a dough has formed—about 2 minutes. Remove dough from the bowl, wrap the dough in plastic wrap and make it flat so it cools quicker. Let it rest and set in the refrigerator for at least 20 minutes.

2. ASSEMBLE, BAKE AND SERVE

Preheat the oven to 300°F (150°C/Gas Mark 2). Lightly flour the bench top. Using a rolling pin, roll the dough to a ¼in (5mm) thickness then cut the shapes—the biscuits should weigh about 2oz (60g) each. Place onto a baking tray lined with baking paper and bake for 15–20 minutes. Remove from oven, set aside to cool, then decorate with chocolate, royal icing or confectionaries of your choice.

GINGERBREAD HOUSE

Gingerbread House

MAKES 1

A special treat for the family at Christmastime is to make your own gingerbread house together. It is simple to make; however, assembly will need to be done in stages to allow the icing to set properly.

2 quantities Gingerbread Dough (see
    Gingerbread People)

17½oz (500g) mixed lollies, jellies and
    chocolate to decorate

ROYAL ICING

Makes 21oz (600g)

 oz (10g) gelatine leaves

3oz (90g) egg whites (about 3 eggs)

17½oz (500g) pure confectioner's/icing sugar

1. PREPARE THE GINGERBREAD DOUGH

Prepare the gingerbread dough following the recipe for Gingerbread People. Using a rolling pin, roll it to a ¼in (5mm) thickness then cut into pieces as per the gingerbread chart. Place the dough pieces onto a baking tray lined with baking paper. Preheat the oven to 300°F (150°C/Gas Mark 2) and bake for 20 minutes to allow the dough to dry out. The drier the biscuit, the longer the house will stay standing. The baked dough should last for 2 weeks at room temperature. Any spare dough can be used to make Gingerbread People, as on previous page.

2. PREPARE THE ROYAL ICING

Only make the royal icing when the house is ready to be assembled.

Place the gelatine leaves in cold water to soften, making sure the leaves are completely submerged. When softened, slightly squeeze out the water and place the gelatine in a small saucepan over a low heat; gently stir until the leaves dissolve into a liquid. Place the egg white and sugar in the bowl of an electric mixer with whisk attachment and slowly beat for 1 minute. Then add the melted gelatine on a slow speed for 1 minute and then on full speed for 3 minutes. The mixture will become soft enough to pipe and will eventually air dry to cement the house together. Put the royal icing into a piping bag with nozzle no. 801 and use the icing as you would use glue. Use the royal icing straightaway or it will become too hard.

EQUIPMENT

Rolling pin

Baking tray

Baking paper

Mixing bowls, 8in (20cm) diameter

Saucepan, 6in (15cm)

Electric mixer with whisk attachment

Piping bag

Piping nozzle no. 801

3. ASSEMBLE THE GINGERBREAD HOUSE

For the walls: Using the royal icing, stick the edge of one wall of the house to the edge of another wall—place against a stable prop as it will take some time to set. Repeat with the remaining walls. Leave the walls to set for at least 2 hours before placing on the roof.

To attach the roof, pipe the royal icing onto the top of the apex and along the top of the rim of the two sides. Attach one roof slat at a time, making sure the top edges line up with the tip of each apex. Repeat to attach the second roof slat in the same manner. If the royal icing is made correctly, the slats will not fall off. If they do, you will need to prop the roof up to hold it, or alternatively hold it in place with your hands, for a few minutes until it begins to set. Ideally, leave the assembled house to set for 2 hours before decorating.

4. TO FINISH AND DECORATE

Attach the front door and chimney. Be creative with decorating using the mixed lollies, jellies and chocolate—use the royal icing to ensure they will stick properly.

GINGERBREAD HOUSE

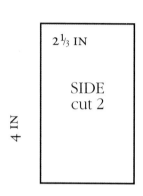

2⅓ IN

SIDE
cut 2

4 IN

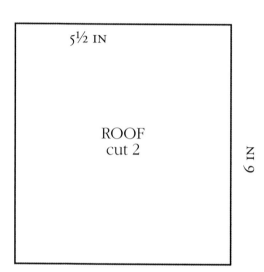

5½ IN

ROOF
cut 2

6 IN

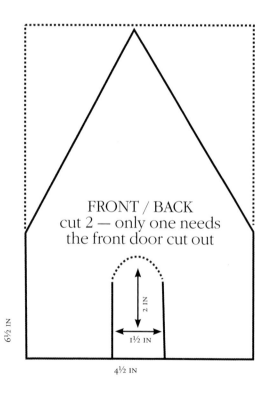

FRONT / BACK
cut 2 — only one needs
the front door cut out

2 IN

6½ IN

1½ IN

4½ IN

CHIMNEY

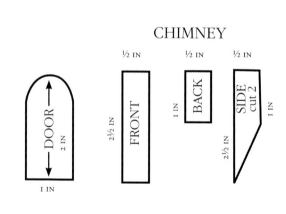

DOOR

2 IN

1 IN

½ IN

FRONT

2½ IN

½ IN

BACK

1 IN

½ IN

SIDE
cut 2

2½ IN

1 IN

Joyeux Noël.

GLOSSARY

Al dente	Cooked so as not to be too soft: firm to the bite
Bain marie	A gentle way to cook or melt ingredients by sitting a bowl over gently simmering water—this is the preferred way to melt chocolate
Baking weights	You can purchase weights at a kitchenware store or create your own by using rice, lentils or beans—see Before you Begin
Blowtorch	A tool used to apply heat to melt sugar on crème brûlée—it is powered by a butane gas canister and is readily available from your local hardware store
Boiling point	When liquid begins to bubble furiously over heat—the water is at 212°F (100°C)
Caramelise	Caramelising is the stage of melting sugar when it starts to colour—can be done with a blowtorch
Coring	To remove the seeds and centre of fruit such as apple or pear
Docking	Spiking holes into a surface with a fork—prevents the dough rising
Egg wash	Beaten whole egg that is used to join pastries together—also gives a golden shine on the top of pastries after baking
Plastic sleeve	A4 size plastic sheet used for chocolate transfers
Prebaked	To partially or fully cook a pastry so that it remains crunchy when a liquid is poured on top
Proving	The final dough rising step before baking
Ribbon stage	It is ribbon stage when the mixture falls in a flat, ribbon-like pattern when drizzled over itself, after beating thoroughly
Score	Making superficial marks on the dough surface
Scraped vanilla bean	Cut the vanilla bean lengthways, open the pod and remove the seeds by scraping with the back of a knife
Sieve	To pass dry or wet ingredients through a fine mesh sieve to remove any lumps
Simmer	To gently cook over a low heat so that the liquid only steams and very slowly bubbles
Skim the surface	To use a ladle or spoon to remove any impurities or bubbles from the surface of a liquid
Soft peak meringue	Egg whites that have been whisked—when the whisk is lifted out of the meringue, it forms a peak and falls back into itself
Soft peak cream	Cream that has been whisked—when the whisk is lifted out of the cream, it forms a peak and falls back into itself

RECIPE INDEX

Index

Acknowledgements

A group of wonderful and talented people have created this book with us. A thank you to our publishers at New Holland, to our stylist Bhavani Konings and our amazing photographer Steve Brown, who have truly brought the recipes to life. To the incredible Kate Fabro, whose support and involvement was unsurpassed every step of the way. Finally, to all our wonderful clients, our greatest supporters, this book is for you, *merci beaucoup.*

About the Authors

Vincent Gardan is a French-born, highly regarded pastry chef with over 25 years experience. Vincent has worked in many Michelin Star restaurants in France and overseas and he received one of his biggest accolades, winning first place in the Ardennes-Eiffel Culinary Prize, at the age of 22.

Michelle Guberina has over 20 years hospitatlity experience in prestigious venues, restaurants and location catering most recently at Patisse Cooking School. As a hands-on business owner, she has a style that few can match.

This paperback edition published in 2014 by
New Holland Publishers
London • Cape Town • Sydney • Auckland
www.newhollandpublishers.com • www.newholland.com.au

First published in 2013.

The Chandlery Unit 114 50 Westminster Bridge Road London SE1 7QY United Kingdom
Wembley Square First Floor Solan Road Gardens Cape Town 8001 South Africa
1/66 Gibbes Street Chatswood NSW 2067 Australia
218 Lake Road Northcote Auckland New Zealand

A catalogue record of this book is available at the British Library and at the National Library of Australia

ISBN: 9781742575926

Managing director: Fiona Schultz
Publisher: Lliane Clarke
Project editor: Jodi De Vantier
Editor: Susin Chow
Designer: Tracy Loughlin
Stylist: Bhavani Konings
Photographer: Steve Brown
Production director: Olga Dementiev
Printer: Toppan Leefung Printing Limited (China)

10 9 8 7 6 5 4 3 2 1

Our thanks to: Ici et La, Waterford Wedgwood, Paper 2, Le Creuset and Côté Maison

Keep up with New Holland Publishers on Facebook and Twitter
www.facebook.com/NewHollandPublishers

UK £19.99
US $16.99